MOTHERS OF THE SAINTS

Easter Weekend 1994
April 1, 2 and 3rd.
Ocean City, Maryland

Mothers of the Saints

Portraits of Ten Mothers of the Saints and Three Saints Who Were Mothers

Wendy Leifeld

Servant Publications
Ann Arbor, Michigan

Acknowledgments for the use of various source materials in
the work are listed in an appendix.

Published by Servant Publications
P.O. Box 8617
Ann Arbor, Michigan 48107

Cover design by Michael Andaloro
Cover photo by SUPERSTOCK, Inc. of the painting
"Mother and Child" by Marie Cassatt

91 92 93 94 95 10 9 8 7 6 5 4 3 2 1

Printed in the United States of America
ISBN 0-89283-678-4

Library of Congress Cataloging-in-Publication Data

Leifeld, Wendy.
    Mothers of saints : portraits of ten mothers of the saints
and three saints who were mothers / Wendy Leifeld.
        p. cm.
    Includes bibliographical references.
    ISBN 0-89283-678-4
    1. Christian saints—Mothers—Biography. 2. Christian
women saints—Biography. 3. Motherhood—Religious
aspects—Christianity.   I. Title.
BR1713.L45 1991
270'.092'2—dc20   90-25417

Dedication

*To the Blessed Virgin, the mother of us all,
and especially to Jane Noble, Patrice Warner,
and Lisa Ferguson for all your encouragement,
and to all mothers everywhere who want to raise godly children.*

Contents

✣ PREFACE ✣

No Saint at This House

THE DAY IS HOT AND HUMID. Two of my children have a touch of flu, or are at least running low fevers and are emotional. All four of them have drifted in and out of the room where I sit at the computer. Questions, always questions. I once heard that people prove their radical capacity to be human because they can always ask another question. I believe it. And it certainly starts at an early age. "Can we play with friends today, Mom?" "What time can we play until?" "Can we have a snack?" "Can we watch *Winnie the Pooh*?" "Do you want to take phone calls?" "What if Dad calls?"

"I'm trying to write this book, can't you see???" I snap after four interruptions in ten minutes. Yes, I am a very human, fallible mother. Here I am writing a book on these holy women, and I am crabbing at my kids. Obviously, studying these women hasn't made me into a saint. But then you probably are not one either, so we can feel comfortable with each other. You may have yelled at your kids today too—or will. "Can't you see I'm reading this book on mothers of the saints? Beat it."

I want you to feel comfortable with these wonderful women I've gotten to know so well. Please, don't get intimidated if they seem too perfect. So much of it goes back to what kind of questions the biographers thought they should answer. In the past, people seemed to want their saints so perfect they seemed inhuman. Nowadays we like

1

to see their humanness because it gives us hope. If we could sit down with any of these ladies over a cup of coffee and a donut (maybe two donuts), they would be the first to tell us all the things the biographers left out or glossed over.

The very reason I wanted to write this book was to introduce you to them because we are all in the same trade: heavy-duty Christian mothering. I suppose we could say they were the professionals, since their children are the proof of the pudding, while we are the amateurs. Just like true aficionados, we can hang around them and try to pick up a few tips, sort of a Christian version of "Learn to Ski with the Pros." Even though I haven't become a saint (ask my husband or kids), I have changed (ditto). Let me tell you about it.

I first met Marie Vianney when I read about her son, the Curé d'Ars. I remember thinking she had a great deal of practical wisdom to offer me as a mother. After that I began to notice that other holy men and women had holy mothers. I began to pay as much attention to Zélie Martin as to her daughter, St. Thérèse of Lisieux. Slowly, I began to amass a stockpile of information on holy mothers that I could draw from as I raised my children. I reexamined some women saints that I was already familiar with for other reasons. I discovered that they were at least as much mothers as reformers, founders, or mystics.

I couldn't just read about them without my thinking beginning to change as well. Motherhood was much *more* than I had previously suspected. More important, for one thing. These mothers really made a difference in their kids' future ability to do God's will. Maybe I could too. Maybe I could act *as if* God wanted my kids to be saints. In that case, I was going to have to take the job more seriously.

All those things I thought were just life, like getting up six times a night with sick children or struggling through daily prayer times as a family, could really have an effect on their lives. I thought they would, I thought they should, then I began to hope that they actually could.

THE JOYFUL CHALLENGE

I was challenged on every level of my being by the character of these women, but they exerted no demand that I change. Rather it was a delightful invitation to join the party. They were certainly having a lot more excitement, joy, and just plain fun being mothers than I had seen anyone else have.

I was challenged to grow in love: in relating to my husband, my children, others, the Virgin Mary, and God himself. To be perfectly frank, I wasn't sure that I wanted to love that much. That was my thought when I first wrote a college paper on holy mothers. All I could give then was a very qualified yes. I find that as I write these pages, the challenge only increases. These women invite us to love totally and to show how sweet it can be to love.

What struck me most was how much they prayed for their children. Their kids were good kids, for the most part; yet woman after woman spent hours in prayer, often in tears, for their children's salvation, for their spiritual well-being. There was a striking similarity between St. Monica, Susanna Wesley, St. Elizabeth Ann Seton, and Maria Kolbe. I saw that I was too nonchalant about the whole affair. "Of course, they'll grow up to love God. After all, we do." I needed to pray more for their salvation. Only in heaven will we see how much was wrought on earth by prayer and prayer alone.

I was challenged to think more deeply about what I was supposed to be doing. I couldn't help noticing that character formation was second only to religious instruction in the priorities of these women. Working with my children's pride or selfishness, their reluctance to help one another, or their eagerness to fight took a lot of time and energy, but I found it was the heart of mothering.

I was challenged to care for the poor, the needy, and the homeless. I have much room for improvement in this area. I saw that it was vitally important that my children care about those who are less fortunate than themselves. They need to learn to give. I have begun to speak out and to write letters for various causes. Christian charity and works of mercy must become an established part of my life and that of my children.

So, do I do even a quarter of the things these women did to raise their children for God? Probably not. I have tried many of their suggestions; some I continue to do. But that isn't the point. If there is one thing that this book tries to state, it is that motherhood is not a static series of do's and don'ts—"Apply these steps to your children and raise a family of saints!" Besides, that would be impossible: Susanna Wesley left her kids awake in their bedrooms, and St. Jeanne de Chantal stayed with them until they fell asleep. Alice of Montbar dressed simply, and St. Margaret of Scotland dressed as beautifully as she could. It just proves that saints aren't saints because they do things exactly alike. Sanctity lies much deeper than that. Motherhood, according to these women, is opposed to legalism.

I have come to understand these women in the same way I understand my other friends. I call Lucia when I need advice about sewing and Carol to find out where the best sales are next week. I get together with Eleanor and talk for hours over a glass of wine. You see what I mean? Take as much or as little advice or interest in each woman in this book as you want, just as you would in real life.

Motherhood is an intensely personal proposition. A relationship where this particular woman, with all her strengths and weaknesses, loves this particular child and does everything in her power to help him or her love God more than she does. St. Monica sure isn't Alice of Montbar, nor is Amy Carmichael much like Maria Kolbe. These women have become my inspiration, not my pattern. I must dare to become the mother God wants of me, and so must you.

These women have become real to me, my friends and prayer partners from heaven. They are not just historical figures but real women who shine like stars in the communion of the saints.

May you, too, find strength, wisdom, and encouragement in reading about the lives of these women. May God bless you and your children.

Feast of the Assumption
August 15, 1990

Holy Motherhood: Shaping the Saints

MOTHERHOOD IS PERHAPS MORE CHALLENGING today than at any time in history. We need to learn everything we can from one another. For example, these three women faced challenges common to many of us. Marie taught her children to share in a way that made a difference in her son's life. Barbe learned a great deal about overcoming a dysfunctional upbringing. Monica was influential in freeing her son from the cult he belonged to for nineteen years.

MARIE: TEACHING UNSELFISHNESS

Marie, a pretty young mother of five, had a common enough problem with her two youngest children. John and Marguerite were eighteen months apart in age and usually played together very well. One day, however, there was a fight. Marguerite grabbed John's treasured rosary from him and ran away. He screamed at her to bring it back, but she only laughed. He caught up with his sister and struggled to wrest it from her fist. Suddenly, crying with all his heart, he ran to Mommy to tell on his sister. She wanted them to learn to share: was she to tell her daughter to give the beads back, or to tell John to let her have them?

BARBE: OVERCOMING THE PAST

Barbe's mother was a harsh, perhaps even a violent woman. Her father was rather formal and distant toward his daughter.

Despite her difficult and lonely childhood, Barbe married Pierre, a hot-tempered tease though a good-hearted man, and had six children. She loved her children immensely but, with her background, would she be a good mother?

In later years, when her daughters were adults, she realized that she had been too exacting and had expected too much from her children. What could she do to correct the past?

MONICA: DEFEATING THE ENEMY

Monica had the same two great sorrows that many women share today: her husband did not believe in God and her eldest son, though brilliant, was wasting away his time, energy, and life in carousing. Not only did he live with a woman and have an illegitimate son, but he also became involved in a strange religious cult.

Neither her son nor her husband would listen to a word she said in defense of the faith, and Monica feared their damnation more than anything else in the world. How could she convince them to become Christians?

These real-life women dealt with problems that we all face as mothers in today's world: sibling squabbles, wayward children, unbelieving husbands, and poor preparation for motherhood. The only difference between them and us is the time in which we live. Marie was the mother of St. Jean-Marie Vianney and lived in the eighteenth century in France. Barbe Acarie was beatified under her religious name, Blessed Marie de l'Incarnation, and lived during the sixteenth century. Monica is a saint of the fourth century, and so is her son Augustine.

Marie wanted to teach Jean (John) something that would last him far longer than a temporary satisfaction over the possession of his rosary beads. She told him to let his sister have them. "Yes, my darling, give them to her for love of the good God." It seems rather hard to ask a four-year-old to give away his most precious possession, but that is exactly what she did. Then, instead of cuddling and comforting him, Marie went to a shelf in the kitchen and took down a small wooden statue of the Blessed Virgin Mary. He had often asked to have it for his very own, and now she gave it to him. He was overjoyed.

Years later this was one of St. Jean's most treasured memories. He dated his tremendous love of the Mother of God from that time.

Barbe Acarie overcame her past by loving her daughters and giving them the time and tenderness her own mother did not give her. Though she still made mistakes, she was able to rectify her past harshness by repenting to her daughters. "I did you much harm, it was very wrong of me." They admitted that she was very strict but assured her that they knew she only intended good for them. A deeper love and unity resulted from her willingness to admit her mistakes.

Because her husband and son were completely closed to anything she said, Monica had no other recourse open to her except prayer. She began to intercede with tears for their conversion. Her husband Patrick was baptized before he died. Years later her son Augustine gave up his cult and, somewhat later, his mistress. Still Monica was not satisfied. She continued to pray and mourn for his salvation. As he moved from town to town she followed him, much to his chagrin. Finally, after nineteen years of prayer, he became a Christian and was baptized. We know him as St. Augustine, one of the greatest Fathers of the Western church. We know her as St. Monica.

MOTHERING THAT MADE A DIFFERENCE

Faith determined how these women would respond to each event in their lives—as wives and as mothers. Their love of God and commitment to be holy parents gives their lives a radiance that shines down through the centuries. By their light we, too, can see a way to be holy mothers in a darkened age.

They offer us a real-life picture of what motherhood can be and the effect it can have on a woman, her husband, her children, and all those who come in contact with her. Because these women operated as if their mothering were their mission from God, they all had a profound influence on the holiness and ministry of their sons and daughters.

Historians credit St. Margaret of Scotland's mothering with producing the best two hundred years of Scottish kings. Some anonymous person wrote on the tomb of Zélie and Louis Martin, the parents of St. Thérèse of Lisieux: "Thank you, dear Christian parents, for giving us a saint to look after us." St. Jean-Marie Vianney, the extraordinary Curé d'Ars, said that his love of prayer, after God, was the work of his dear mother.

These mothers show us, in obscure and dramatic ways, the holiness that is possible and feasible in the married state of life. Not all of them are canonized, but all of them evidenced the deep piety and works of mercy that characterized their famous children.

The personal strength and character of each of these holy women expands our vision of what is possible for the married state of life. Many of the practical ways they mothered their children may be as helpful as their lives are inspiring.

WHAT THIS BOOK OFFERS AND HOW TO USE IT

For the purpose of this book, I have limited myself to exploring the women as mothers only. Several of them could be written about just as extensively as holy wives. All of them are fully women with many aspects to them. Many of the fathers could be the subject of a book such as this one. I have blithely ignored their relationships with their husbands and any major personal accomplishments, concentrating instead on the mothering of their children.

Not all of these women were Catholic. Susanna Wesley was an Anglican and the mother of the founder of Methodism, John Wesley, and the great hymn writer Charles Wesley. Amy Carmichael, a Protestant missionary to India, mothered hundreds of orphaned, abused, or abandoned children. In the spirit of true ecumenism, certainly the motherly example of these two Christian women is worth considering. Their love of God in raising children can be inspiring and informative to Catholics and Protestants alike.

Further, while most of these women had children who have been canonized by the Catholic church, some of them are saints in their own right. In this book, I have classified these women as follows:

Mothers of the Saints

- Maria Kolbe, mother of St. Maximilian Kolbe;
- Marie Vianney, mother of St. Jean-Marie Vianney the Curé d'Ars;
- Zélie Martin, mother of St. Thérèse of Lisieux;
- St. Monica, mother of St. Augustine of Hippo and a saint in her own right;
- St. Margaret of Scotland, mother of St. David—a saint by popular custom and a line of holy Scottish kings (also a saint in her own right);
- Alice of Montbar, mother of St. Bernard of Clairvaux and six lesser known saints.
- Susanna Wesley, mother of two great men of God— John and Charles Wesley—known for their love of God and invaluable contributions to Christianity;
- Margarita Bosco, the mother of St. John Bosco;

- Amy Carmichael, adoptive mother to hundreds of Indian children whom she led to Christ.
- Assunta Goretti, the mother of St. Maria Goretti.

Saints Who Were Mothers

- Barbe Acarie; (beatified under Marie de l'Incarnation, her religious name)
- St. Jeanne-Françoise de Chantal;
- St. Elizabeth Ann Seton.

Full length books have been written about many of these women. The lives of those mothers known only through their famous children, however, must be pieced together through many different books about their offspring. In both cases, several of the best books are either out-of-print, hard to locate, or in foreign languages. This book is an attempt to introduce you to them in hopes that you will pursue further acquaintance through additional reading. A suggested reading list at the end of the book highlights the more readily available books.

Although these mothers have a great many things in common, I have emphasized only the aspect of each woman that is particularly relevant to Christian motherhood today. All the chapters are self-contained and can be read in any order.

This book can be used as the basis for a women's study group or for individual reading. The practical pointers titled "For Your Life," which are listed at the end of the chapters, recall some of the notable, concrete ways each mother used to bring her children to God. They are there for your review or to initiate small group discussion. If you decide to apply some of the practical pointers, I advise that you only take one pointer at a time for several weeks. That way you and your children will have time to incorporate the practical wisdom into your daily lives. Otherwise, your attempts to apply the pointers will probably prove frustrating and ultimately futile.

In my own life, I have been inspired by the way Marie Vianney took the time to explain the Mass over and over to her son, Jean-Marie. Now whenever any of my kids asks me questions about what is going on during Mass, I'm much more inclined to take the time to explain, instead of hushing them up and waiting until after Mass. This is but one of many practical pointers that I've gleaned from these women's lives.

Keep in mind that this is just a selection of mothers of saints and saints who were mothers. Saints Frances of Rome, Bridget of Sweden, Margaret Clitherow, Blessed Anna-Marie Taigi, and many others are also women who were married and raised their children for Christ.

We live in an exciting and challenging age. In the secular world, family life is under attack and motherhood can be looked down upon. Yet in the church there is a new appreciation and understanding of married holiness and the importance of Christian parents as never before in history. Our "big sisters" in the communion of the saints are willing to help us by their prayers and example to lead a new generation to Christ.

ONE

"A Love Stronger Than Death" Maria Kolbe

By all accounts it is very difficult to become a saint, even with the grace of God, but this twentieth-century woman teaches us how difficult it is to be a mother of a saint.

THE YEAR IS 1941. The place, Hitler's Poland, a devastated, war-consumed land. A white-haired, heavyset woman in Cracow agonizes over her son's imprisonment at Auschwitz. Two years before, her son was the famous Franciscan priest, editor, publisher, and founder of Niepokalanów. How she had worried then! Was he getting enough sleep? Was he taking the time to eat and rest? Was he remembering to wear the sweater she knit him? Would he work himself to the point of collapse again? Now those worries seemed trivial in comparison to her current fears.

"There seems little hope of Father Maximilian's return [from Auschwitz], and an exhausting battle erupts inside me," Maria Kolbe wrote to the friars at Niepokalanów on April 14, 1941. "I want to accept the will of God, yet I am violently assaulted with temptations. How is it that others are answered and fulfilled in their prayers, while I experience the opposite? The more I pray, the more bitter are the results.

"I was tempted to forsake my trust in the protection of the Immaculate Mother. I am tormented; my son was faithful to her and she does not help him . . . she does not save him. I am overcome with remorse . . . I hear [the Virgin Mary] speak to my heart, the greater grace is to know how to suffer, rather than passively accept suffering. I grieve because of my attitude toward the fairest of Mothers.

"Physical and spiritual agony engulfs me. If my son were to die in Niepokalanów, I would at least know where he is buried. Although with joy I would give my life for his ransom, I fear to pray impetuously for his release. I am inspired to pray for what is most important—his sanctification and the glory of God.

"Vehemently and with conviction I begged, as a mother who really loves her children, for Maximilian the strong love of martyrs. A love stronger than death—love that allows one to face death with joy. I listen with a torn heart to an inner voice that whispers, 'above natural love, one must place the love of God, and the desire for eternal happiness for those we love.' "[1]

Four months later, to the day, Fr. Maximilian Kolbe will finally die after sacrificing his life to save another. Maria must endure weeks of rumors before the truth is confirmed: he truly is dead. She suffers alone, in solitude and silence. April comes again before her emotions catch up with her faith, and she can finally experience the peace and serenity of surrender.

Her son's crowning triumph was her crucible of faith. His imprisonment and martyrdom were the final affirmation of his continual yes to God. For Maria, it was the ultimate test of her lifelong faithfulness to the Lord. Both suffered for love; both triumphed in love.

After his death, the Franciscans at Niepokalanów asked Maria to write down everything she could remember about

Father Maximilian's childhood. She was ready, then, to remember, and in remembering him, to remember her whole life.

Maria Dąbrowska was born February 25, 1870, in Zduńska Wola, Poland. That area of Poland was occupied by Russia, and every effort was made to eradicate the Polish language, history, and culture. Maria's parents were weavers by trade, as were most of the inhabitants of the town. She grew up with both parents working at the looms fourteen hours a day. Maria was able to finish her elementary education at school before she took her place in the family's business.

Even as a child Maria loved God and the Blessed Virgin Mary. She and her younger sister, Anna, loved to pray by the family altar and play "church" with their little friends. Maria grew up longing to be a nun, but the Russians had suppressed the Roman Catholic church in the sector of Poland in which she lived. Because she felt that the door to the religious life was closed, she decided to marry the most devout man she could find.

She found him in Julius Kolbe, a cheerful, friendly, handsome man a year younger than herself. His strong faith and annual participation in the eleven-day walking pilgrimage to Czestochowa were what attracted her, however. They sincerely loved one another and married on October 5, 1891.

Together they set up looms in a small rented home not far from the church in town. The crucified Christ and an icon of Our Lady of Czestochowa hung in the family prayer corner, along with pictures of the special saints and patrons of the family. Every family had such a place called the "Honorary Corner." It served as a constant reminder that God was a part of the family's life and activities, and a continual invitation to seek his protection and blessing.

Maria gave birth to a son, Francis, on July 25, 1892. Immediately after the baby was born, Julius greeted his wife with a blessing, "*Bóg Ci wielki zapłać* [May God richly reward you.]'' From the moment she knew the child was a boy she determined that he was going to be a priest. Eighteen months later a little brother, Raymond, was born on January 8, 1894. Julius and Maria decided this son would carry on the business and support them in their old age. Both babies were baptized the day they were born. Raymond was nicknamed *Mundek* and one day would take the name Maximilian in religious life.

Julius and Maria joined the Third Order of St. Francis in 1894. Little did they realize how the rest of their life would be interwoven with the Franciscans until every one of the family became part of the pattern.

When the Industrial Revolution finally hit Eastern Europe, the cottage weavers were driven out of work by the textile factories springing up in the large towns. Julius moved the family to Lodz and went to work in a mill while Maria stayed home with the boys. In 1896 a third son, Joseph, was born.

The city environment was unbearable after the loveliness of their native town. Julius and Maria agreed that it was no place to raise their sons and moved to Pabianice, a smaller factory town.

The two of them opened a shop in their home, selling food and housewares to factory workers on their way home from work. They worked on a home loom and gardened until the shop was successful. Life was finally comfortable for the Kolbes, but not for long. In 1898 their fourth son, Valentine, died at twelve months and then in 1904, Anthony, their fifth son, died at age four.

In that same year, Russia slumped into a severe economic depression. The Japanese-Russian War only made matters worse as strikes and protests against the working conditions in the factories, as well as governmental intolerance and oppression mounted. Poland groaned under occupation and began to struggle for freedom again. The Kolbes' little shop was finally forced into bankruptcy. Julius then began to organize factory workers in protests. They printed a clandestine publication and passed it from hand to hand. Even young Raymond drew Polish eagles on a public wall, for which he was rebuked by Mama. She was displeased by his imprudence, not his patriotism. After all, Julius had already been put in jail once, and she could not bear the thought of her son also being caught by the police.

Maria worked in the factory during this difficult time, but she made a point of being available to the neighborhood women as a midwife. When her skill was not enough in life-threatening situations, Maria resorted to prayer for the mother and child.

HOLINESS IS LOVE, NOT PERFECTION

A complex person by nature, Maria was like a loaf of homemade bread: crusty on the outside and soft within, wholesome and heartwarming and down-to-earth. Julius was the indulgent one and Maria, much stricter. She was a good friend to other women and close to her sister Anna. Compassionate to women in labor, she could be sensitive and gentle when all was not right with the child or the birth. She exuded confidence, determination, and control, yet she had moments of numbing insecurity about her mothering.

Although she was a competent homemaker, she envied other women's skill in that area. Maria had such a high ideal of what a Christian mother and wife should be and do that she never felt that she could measure up to it. At different points in her life she felt that she was a failure. Years later when the heroic sanctity of her son was evident to all, Maria denied having any role in its formation: "I felt my inadequacy and begged the Mother of God to substitute for me."[2] She could not see the good she brought forth in her children; any good results were solely due to her children's cooperation with the grace of God.

As a result of her insecurity, Maria was compulsive about order in the home, cleanliness, and being on time. She was a perfectionist. She worried constantly over her sons: their progress, characters, futures. She was overprotective and possessive. Yet her personal struggle with insecurity did not prevent her from living a devout life or her children from becoming holy.

If love can cover a multitude of sins, it surely must cover our weakness and failings as well. We can feel that our own faults must irreparably scar our children for life. We can feel just as insecure about the job we are doing as mothers. How can we be good mothers when we are not perfect ourselves?

The Kolbe family beautifully reveals that the seedbed of holiness is love, not perfection of personality. Maria's life can give us a great deal of hope: despite our personal struggles, our children, by the grace of God, can become holy adults. And so can we—if, like Maria, we use our very weakness to drive us closer to God.

Maria turned to prayer when she was feeling insecure as a mother. She asked Mary, the Mother of God, to mother her sons and make up to them what was lacking. Her realization of her own real and imagined failings brought her to rely more and more on the grace of God for her own life. The Eucharist was very important to her as a source of that grace, but even more so as intercession for her family. The rosary was another means she used to turn to Jesus through his Mother Mary to help her sons and husband.

Both Julius and Maria taught the boys at home for the first several years. An elementary education cost a great deal of money which the family simply did not have. In any case, each family had to teach the forbidden Polish history, literature, and language in secret. Not all learning was academic, however. Julius loved the tales of knights and heroes, saints and statesmen, and brought an excitement to the lessons that inspired his sons. Raymond was caught up with the idea of knighthood, an idea that would become foundational to his mission in life, to be a knight for the Immaculate Mary.

The boys had their chores to do besides their schoolwork and were assigned additional reading in their spare time. They played with their friends, and Francis taught himself to play the organ and piano.

When Francis was about twelve his parents decided to make the financial commitment of further schooling in hopes that he would one day be a priest. Raymond was to stay at home, help his mother with his younger brother Joseph, and perhaps in two years go on to school as well. Providence intervened, however; the neighboring pharmacist decided to tutor Raymond, and he caught up with his older brother's studies.

In 1907 the boys had the opportunity to leave their home and move to Lvov to attend minor seminary. At first, Julius and Maria would not consider Raymond's going with Francis. They had other plans for him, but through prayer his parents came to believe it was God's will for their son. The boys were smuggled out of Russian Poland under a load of hay and began a new life in Austrian Poland.

The first years of seminary life were fulfilling and enjoyable for both Francis and Raymond, but toward the end of their time in minor seminary Raymond lost his desire to be a priest. He thought he was too independent and too much a free-thinker to be happy in religious life. Just as he and Francis were on the way to tell the superior they were leaving, their mother arrived for a visit. She had news for them, news that altered their plans drastically.

Joseph, their little brother, would join them at the Franciscan monastery since he, too, wanted to be a priest. That was surprising but understandable. The next piece of news was shocking and disturbing for the boys and for us, as modern readers as well. Julius, their father, had agreed to let Maria leave him and go to a convent. They would never again live together as man and wife.

TO SERVE GOD ABOVE ALL OTHERS

"How can this be God's will?" we ask. Everything that is known about the Kolbes shows that their home life was ideal, their marriage sincere. Our resounding question is, "Why?" Why did Julius allow her to go? Why did she feel she had to? Her action can seem dishonorable and strike us as if she broke her sacramental vows of marriage. There are no clear answers available, and it will always remain a mystery of love, for that is ultimately what it was.

Maria had originally wanted to be a sister. She only chose marriage because she thought it was impossible to join an order. At that time in history, marriage was not seen as an equal call to holiness. In her defense, it must be stated that Maria could have remained single but thought that married life better served God than a single life in the world. For seventeen years they had had a good marriage, and she had loved and still loved her husband.

Now that her children had entered the seminary, she longed to dedicate the remainder of her life to serving the Lord in a convent. Julius planned to join a monastery as well after he had paid off their debts and completed Joseph's education.

Julius lived out a foreshadowing of his son's heroic martyrdom. He loved Maria and his family life. From this point on he would suffer loneliness, poverty, and isolation, never finding another place that felt like home to him. His love for his wife was so great that her happiness meant more to him than his, and so he let her go. This self-sacrifice for another's well-being and life would be duplicated, but not bettered, by his son Raymond.

Raymond took his mother's news as a divine sign that he was to become a priest. Both he and Francis were received as novices of the Order of Friars Minor Conventual on September 4, 1910. Francis was given the name Valerian and Raymond, Maximilian from the Roman Martyrology. They moved to Cracow to continue their studies where their father joined them as the monastery's handyman for a short while.

Maria joined the Benedictine Sisters as an extern affiliate in Lvov, just down the street from where her youngest son lived. She stayed there for five years until she was convinced that she belonged, like her sons, in the Franciscan family. Eventually, in 1913, Maria joined the Felician Sisters in Cracow to live and work with them without the possibility of becoming a nun. Here she remained until her death thirty-three years later.

Maria lived in the parlor area, outside the enclosure in the convent, and took on any duty her superiors assigned her. She would deliver messages, pick up parcels, pay the bills, and take care of any outside business for the convent. Now she had the time to devote to prayer, especially adoration before the Blessed Sacrament. A favorite job of hers was to cut the communion wafers. Unpaid and without savings, she lived by God's providence.

Brother Maximilian had been sent to Rome to study in 1912. Brother Valerian lived close by at the Franciscan Monastery, and Joseph was still in Lvov. August 3, 1914, changed their peaceful existence and plans forever as World War I broke around them and redefined their lives and nation. Brother Valerian left the monastery in order to enlist, and Julius became a commander in a reconnaissance unit.

No news was heard of Julius for many years, but Francis (Brother Valerian) was hospitalized with an inflammation of the leg bone before ever seeing battle. Considered to be incurable, he was discharged from the army and thought to be unfit for religious life as well. He decided to marry, but he hid the news from Maria.

She wrote to Joseph, now called Brother Alphonse, "It seems to me that (Brother Valerian's) leg is a little better. He is able to bend it quite well. Perhaps the Lord will still comfort us; we both have a hope that if God heals him, He will also assist him to return to the monastery. While waiting for this miraculous rebirth, I would willingly sacrifice everything and joyously accept death, if this would help, for Valerian's reform, and for your and Maximilian's perseverance."[3]

Maria was to be disappointed. Francis married Irene Triebling in 1917. The picture and announcement he sent to both Brother Alphonse and Maria was met with anger and criticism. She refused to accept his actions. He was supposed to be a priest, she believed, and now she feared for his salvation. Francis and Irene soon stopped receiving the sacraments. This only gave Maria more ammunition for her reproaches.

FAITHFUL IN THE MIDST OF DISAPPOINTMENT

Maria was unable to reconcile her plan for her son with his interpretation of God's will for his life. She struggled with guilt—it must be her fault that he could not persevere in his vocation—and could not let go. Both Brothers Alphonse and Maximilian came to terms with Francis' decision years before Maria was able to be at peace.

All this served to drive her ever more into the arms of Christ, especially finding solace in her love for the Virgin Mary. She redoubled her prayers for her sons, all of them. From now on her overriding concern for her sons would be for them to remain faithful to their Franciscan profession and to attain a great though hidden sanctity. Here too, God would not answer her prayers as she prayed them. Their holiness would exceed her imagination and it would be revealed, not hidden, in Maximilian's case, to astonish the world and glorify God.

His brother's marriage convinced Brother Alphonse that he must rely only on God in order to be a good and faithful religious. He wrote to his mother that he depended more and more on her prayers and sacrifices to obtain God's mercy.

The war continued to ravage Europe while Maria fought her internal battles. Maximilian, while in Rome, conceived the idea of a movement of renewal with the Mother of God as the guiding force and began the Confraternity of Mary Immaculate in late 1917. This "Militia" was an "army" composed of laymen and religious dedicated to spiritual warfare and renewal of the church. It was dedicated to the Immaculata, his favorite name for the Mother of God. This became his life's work. On April 28, 1918, he was ordained a priest.

The family, separated by the war and duty, was held together by Maria's prayers. Through frequent letters she made her love, her joy, and her prayers known to them, and theirs to her.

After the war was over, the family finally found out the fate of their father. His entire company had been captured by the Russians in 1914, and because he was an officer he was hanged.

Maria found a new avenue for the love in her heart, a host of daughters that she never bore, in the postulants and candidates for the order. She encouraged them, helped them in a multitude of ways, and prayed for them. They learned to love this stolid woman who lived on the outskirts of their lives. Her unofficial work among these women and her duties in the convent took up the bulk of her time, but there was always time for her sons when they came to visit. She, like so many mothers, did not feel it was often enough.

Maximilian returned to Poland and in 1920 fell gravely ill and had to spend months in the mountains recuperating. Shortly after that, Alphonse came down with communicable tuberculosis and had to be isolated from everyone else. Maria's first concern was his lack of warm clothing, so she stayed up all night in order to knit him a scarf and warm socks. In the morning she went to the train station to see him off. Though terribly concerned for his life, she entrusted him to the Mother of God. He recovered and was ordained with the rest of his class.

Francis and Irene had a baby daughter, and Maria went to visit. Francis had forgiven the family long before and had initiated all the reconciliation efforts; despite this, his relationship with his mother was still strained and painful. She was so deeply hurt and angry that only God working through the passage of time would be able to heal her heart. She saw Francis and Irene's marital problems and even separation as a confirmation that she was right, that he had not done God's will. Alphonse and Maximilian both worked to help Maria forgive and accept her son and his wife. Alphonse wrote, "Your letter was sad. What am I to do?—explain the will of God?—you are convinced of it! Tell you to pray? Mama, you taught me how! Instead I will write peaceful letters; let Christ do the rest. You will receive holy peace and our loss will somehow be rewarded."[4]

Maria struggled and suffered because she loved Francis, not because she hated him. Ultimately, her love for him would triumph, but God would use the death of one son to heal the relationship with the other.

In 1922 the first copy of the magazine *Knight of the Immaculata* was published, but Maria was dubious about Maximilian's involvement and the great financial and personal cost of the effort. This venture too led her to pray all the more for her sons. It was only when the publication began to prove successful that she was able to support it wholeheartedly. In fact, she began to sell subscriptions and to talk up the "Militia" to anyone she could corner for a minute.

The work was so successful that the Franciscans built a city for the Immaculata, Niepokalanów, where the publishing house was centered. Maximilian and Alphonse were deeply involved in every aspect of the work there, and in 1927 the city was blessed and dedicated by the provincial superior.

Maximilian went to Japan in 1930, leaving Alphonse in charge of the Marian work in Europe. Four weeks after arriving in Japan the friars printed the first edition of *Knight of the Immaculata* in Japanese, and the pace of missionary activity only picked up from there.

Less than a year later, Alphonse died of appendicitis just before surgery. Francis' whereabouts were unknown, and Maximilian was in Japan. Maria was left alone to bear the sudden shock and pain of her youngest son's unexpected death. Maximilian wrote to her, "He lived, suffered, and sacrificed himself for the Immaculata."[5]

Maria was beginning to know loneliness: she missed her husband and children at the traditional breaking of the Christmas wafer. Her sister Anna tried to comfort her by letter. Maria did not understand the reason, but she was able to accept her son's death as the will of God.

As she grieved for her son she experienced some hostility and jealousy from the Felician Sisters in the neighboring convents who disliked a laywoman carrying out the convent's business. Perhaps this additional suffering served to distract Maria from her grief and disappointments.

Maximilian returned to Poland in 1936 to become superior of Niepokalanów. Over seven hundred Franciscans lived there, the largest Catholic religious community in the world and the largest publishing house in Poland. Their apostolate continued to spread rapidly. The publication, *Knight of the Immaculata*, was reaching over a million subscribers a month, and several other magazines and newspapers had joined it. In addition to the publishing apostolate, the friars began a radio broadcast in 1938. Niepokalanów, and specifically Fr. Maximilian Kolbe, became a major force of public opinion in Poland.

WORLD WAR II AND A MISSION FULFILLED

At the height of Niepokalanów's success, Poland was invaded. Fr. Kolbe had used his apostolate to speak out against the Nazis and knew the friars were in danger. Most of them were disbanded and sought safer hiding places, but Fr. Maximilian was ordered by his superiors to remain. Around thirty-six brothers and some priests stayed with him at Niepokalanów. The Gestapo arrived twelve days after the invasion of Poland and arrested Fr. Maximilian and all but two brothers. They took them to prison in Ametitz, Germany.

Maria remained in Cracow. Refugees and Felician sisters from Warsaw and other towns found their way to the convent, but Maria heard no word about the fate of Niepokalanów for weeks. Finally she heard about her son's imprisonment only to hear that he had been released on the feast of the Immaculate Conception.

Was this God's gentle way of helping her prepare for his eventual death? Did this first incarceration help her to bear the second and final one? Surely, in retrospect, we can see how having to bear the grievous blows of Fr. Alphonse's death and Fr. Maximilian's imprisonment must have trained her to shoulder the heavier weight of his martyrdom. Her severe disappointment and struggle to accept her first son's decision for his life helped her to accept God's decision to take her second son's life.

Niepokalanów had been plundered by the Gestapo in the friar's absence and was made into a detention camp. Fr. Maximilian adjusted easily to the changes, began charitable outreaches, and instituted all-day adoration before the Blessed Sacrament to pray for world peace and in thanksgiving that the buildings still stood in the city of the Immaculata.

Meanwhile Francis had escaped capture, and after weeks of wandering ended up back in Zduńska Wola. His wife and child spent the first part of the war in the area under Russian occupation until Francis managed to bring them to his hometown.

Fr. Maximilian was once again arrested on February 17,

1941, and sent first to Pawiak, a prison in Warsaw, and then on to Auschwitz. Because he was a priest he was treated more cruelly than others. Fr. Maximilian believed that he had been sent to the concentration camp by the Immaculata, with a mission to fulfill.

Maximilian only sent one letter to Maria and it was on the regulation camp form. He told her that he was faring well. "Be at peace Mother, and do not worry about me or my health. God is everywhere. He watches over all and everything with great love...." He carefully omitted any mention of the frequent beatings, the times the guard dogs were set upon him, the near starvation conditions, his bout of pneumonia in Pawiak prison. Better that she did not know these things.

Maria found relief from her anxieties and consolation for her heart in caring for others. The Felician sisters hid priests, took in many other nuns forced out of their convents, and fed the refugees. Maria Kolbe took part in all the work and continued to run her errands for the Superior. Now more than ever Maria prayed: prayer for her sons, prayer for the country, prayer for the world; prayer for everyone she met occupied her time.

Two months after Fr. Maximilian wrote to her, he was dead. His perseverance in Christian charity and character was complete up until the moment they injected him with carbolic acid. Maria's continual prayers for perseverance were abundantly answered. She was told he volunteered to give his life to save another's. Only after the war, in 1945, would more details be known and would she fully comprehend that he was not just a martyr but a saint. Loss, sheer, unmitigated loss, racked her very being. The superior of Niepokalanów sent her remembrances of her son: a photograph of him, his rosary beads, the last article he wrote, and some hair from the beard he had in the Orient. They only augmented her pain in those days.

Julius was dead, Fr. Alphonse was dead, Francis had

denied his vocation and was unhappy in his marriage, and Fr. Maximilian was dead. She suffered intensely. Strangely, and providentially, it was Francis, her black sheep, who came to her comfort. "Mama, he is better off than we are," Francis wrote, "He has accomplished his goals and in the way he dreamt. Mama, you have no right to be sad. You should be filled with holy envy and rejoice that all worked out for him.

"Of course the wound aches—the wound of self, and the wound of family bonds. For the family is one body with many members. If one member is cut off the entire body suffers. . . ."[6]

Francis refused to let his mother remain uncomforted and wrote again: "Why mother of sorrows? Does not God reign? Was it not his will what had happened? . . . Mama, raise higher than weak self pity. I know it hurts, but he is the happiest of our whole family. Should we carry this sorrow in our hearts because Raymond obtained the height of his holy dream? You are Mama, 'Mother most happy,' Is this not true? Raymond has made you what I have pointed out. Please God, that such a fate does not find my path. . . ."[7]

THE POWER OF PRAYER AND THE MERCY OF SUFFERING

Finally, as the long winter of war and grief ends, Maria was at last at peace with God's will for her son's life. Francis wrote to her again, "I am pleased that you have come to grips with the fact of Raymond's death and your peace has returned. I understand that it takes a magnanimous spirit to give up your cherished child and admit he is the possession of the Lord."[8]

What she could not do for Francis, admit that he belonged to the Lord, she finally could do for Fr. Maximilian—and, consequently, Francis. The war and devastation brought a new peace and reconciliation between the two of them—perhaps the first miracle of St. Maximilian. When Francis comforted his mother, her heart was healed toward him.

Francis had joined the underground resistance in the war. In 1943 he was arrested and held at Litzmannstadt. He was sent to Auschwitz, then on to the concentration camps at Buchenwald, Sachsenhausen, and Mittelbau.

Aniela, her granddaughter, wrote to Maria of her father's fate. Her son, so recently refound, was now lost to her but not to God. She was able to respond to his imprisonment with faith and confidence in God's mercy. These personal sufferings transformed Maria into a harp of human sufferings. She vibrated with each person's anguish and ceaselessly echoed it in prayer. Compassion radiated from her to all she met. The driving, domineering woman of the past had been changed by suffering into a gentle image of Christ's love.

Francis wrote to his mother from Buchenwald to request packages of food and to assure her of his well-being. It was the last letter she would receive from her last living son. Just months before the end of the war, Francis Kolbe died in the camps. Irene Kolbe died of the grippe months after her husband. Maria grieved and wanted reassurance that her daughter-in-law had been at peace with God when she died.

Maria's last years were lived out peacefully, prayerfully given to the service of the Felician Sisters. On March 17, 1946, on the way to a meeting of the Third Order Franciscans, Maria stumbled and fell in the street. A priest from the Capuchin monastery was summoned and anointed her as she died. Her last words were, "My son! My son!"

Maria Kolbe was mother of a saint, but not perfect herself. Mother of a martyr, she suffered intensely to surrender him to God's care. How easy it is in the safety and peace of our suburban homes to desire that our children be true lovers of God when they grow up! How difficult it is when God takes us at our word! It was a journey that took Maria to the depths of her faith, even as her son was raised on high. It is perilous to pray for our children to be saints. Who knows? God might take us up on it and we, too, must yield to the designs of God for our children.

Maria taught her sons to pray. Witness after witness testified that Fr. Maximilian was constantly praying and leading others to prayer. Prayer was the source of his strength and the transforming power among those in the concentration camp and later in the starvation bunker where he met his end. Many women have taught their children to read and write as Maria did. When she taught them to pray, however, she gave them a gift that only grew greater as all else was stripped away.

Was there any truth in Maria's feelings of inadequacy and inferiority? The answer must be yes, it cannot be otherwise. Her great love for her sons and her great faith, however, triumphed over her weakness. Maria found the answer for her inherent human imperfections in the power of God and the love of the Blessed Virgin.

No mother can be everything for her children, no mother can be perfect, yet each mother can find the same answer to her own failings as Maria did. We can always pray and yield to God's mercy.

❧ FOR YOUR LIFE ❧

- Crucifixes and pictures of saints displayed in a prominent place at home can be a constant reminder that God is part of our family life.

- Maria's own realization of her weaknesses and faults led her to pray more and to seek the graces available in the sacraments.

- Maria's life stresses that we can never pray too much for our children.

TWO

"After God It Was the Work of My Dear Mother"
Marie Vianney

Marie Vianney was just a peasant woman, but her deep devotion and mothering profoundly affected the future Curé d'Ars, St. Jean-Marie Vianney.

THOUSANDS OF PILGRIMS stood in line, sometimes for days, in order to have the Curé d'Ars hear their confessions. Every day hundreds packed the church, while the rest stood in the square outside to hear his famous eleven o'clock catechism lesson. His prophetic insight and clarity were talked about all over France. His love of prayer and the sacraments was extraordinary.

People would often congratulate Jean-Marie on his love of prayer and the church, which had begun so early in life. "After God, I owe it to my mother; she was so good!" he would respond with tears in his eyes. "Virtue passes readily from the heart of a mother into that of her children." Over and over during his life, he gave the credit for his beginnings of sanctity to his mother.[1]

Marie Beluse married Matthieu Vianney on February 11, 1778, in Ecully, a tiny village not far from Lyon. Nothing is known of her childhood and very little of her life, except how it affected her son. No faults are recorded of her, not because she did not have any but because they were not important in the eyes of her son's biographers. She was a good, solid woman of peasant stock. Uneducated but possessing shrewd and deep wisdom, she was a good spouse for Matthieu. He was gruff and stubborn but generous and hard-working. He had a faith that kept him steady with his eyes fixed on the needs at hand and the tumultuous times ahead. His wife's faith, just as solid, could also look beyond the present moment and soar.

Jean-Marie was born into a heritage of generous hospitality. His grandfather Pierre Vianney opened his house every evening to beggars. They would sit at the family table and were the first to be served, then they would pray with the family and sleep above the bakehouse. One of those guests was a young man by the name of Benoît Labre, the saintly wayfarer. Labre wrote Vianney a letter thanking him for his hospitality. This letter from the saint was treasured in the family and passed down to Jean-Marie.

Marie married into this tradition of hospitality and continued it. It was no small thing to be ready to serve upwards of sixteen extra men every evening in addition to your own family. Not only food but also clothing was handed out by Marie. She often did extra mending or sewing to supply the generous gestures of her husband and son. Care and love for the poor were passed on to the children as if by osmosis: they had never known anything else.

Pierre and Marie had six children, and every one of them was dedicated to the Virgin Mary before they were born. Catherine; Jeanne-Marie, who died at age five; François, the oldest son and future heir; Jean-Marie; Marguerite or Gothon as she was affectionately called; and another

François known as Cadet. Jean-Marie was born on May 8, 1786, at about midnight. The midwife declared that he would either be a great saint or a great sinner. All of the children were born at home where a picture of the Blessed Mother hung over their parents' bed.

Marie had made a secret vow to consecrate their second son to the service of the altar and named him Jean-Baptiste-Marie accordingly.

The Vianney farmhouse was on the edge of Dardilly, a small village in the east of France. Mount Blanc loomed in the distance. Matthieu owned several acres of land and farmed it with his family. There were pastures, vineyards, fields of crops, and the woods. It is possible that no other saint has been so deeply affected by his childhood sur-roundings. The sermons and counsels of the Curé are full of the commonplace analogies familiar to his audience. He speaks of vines in bloom, smoke rising from wood fires, corn growing to harvest.

The love of parents for their children and children for their parents are significant images for him of the love of God the Father and Mary, and our love for them: "When he sees us coming, he leans his heart very low towards his little creature, just like a father who bends down to listen to his little child speaking to him." "The Virgin Mary is like a mother who has many children and is continually occupied in going from one to another." He had learned well about the gift of love in his family and through it could understand the mystery of God's love for us.

This gift of explaining profound spiritual matters in the simplest language he learned from his mother. Before he was a year old, she would take his hand in hers and show him how to make the sign of the cross. She taught him to fold his hands in prayer. Like many other Catholic children, he learned to say the names of Jesus and Mary by the time he was eighteen months old. As she went about her work in the house, or as they walked to the fields and worked around the farmyard, she spoke about the faith to her children. He learned his first prayers this way.

She tried to go to daily Mass whenever she could. When she brought Jean, she would put him in front of her and explain what the priest was doing. Jean learned, like his mother, to "bless the hour"; cross himself, recite a Hail Mary, and then cross himself again.

In the evening, Marie would sit beside the fire while Jean swept the floor where the beggars had sat. His sister Catherine, as devout as he was, stayed up with him, and his mother would tell them Bible stories. Just before bed they recited prayers for the suffering souls in Purgatory, then Marie would tuck the children into bed. She would talk of Jesus, Mary, and the guardian angels to focus their thoughts on God before they went to sleep. In the morning she was the one to wake the children to make sure their first thought would be of God.

Catherine and Jean were very much like their mother in their deep devotion. It is natural that she would spend as much time explaining and sharing her love of God with them as she could.

One day as Jean-Marie and Gothon (as Marguerite was affectionately called), were playing, they started to fight over a rosary. It was Jean-Marie's prize possession, and under no circumstances was she going to get it away from him. They screamed at each other and began to tussle when suddenly Jean-Marie broke away and ran to his mother crying. He thought to enlist her support, but instead she told him to give the beads to his sister. "Yes, my darling, give them to her for love of the good God." Jean-Marie cried harder than ever but gave Gothon the beads.

As a reward for his sacrifice, Marie gave him a small wooden statue of the Blessed Mother that he had long admired. "Oh! How I loved that statue, neither by day nor by night would I be parted from it. I should not have slept had I not had it beside me in my little bed. . . . The Blessed Virgin was the object of my earliest affections; I loved her even before I knew her."

Pierre went very early to the fields, and after the children completed the home chores, they joined him. By the time Jean-Marie was seven, he and Gothon were sent off to tend the sheep and cows. They took their knitting with them. Both boys and girls in those days knitted stockings for the family while shepherding.

Once a neighbor asked Marie if her son thought he was the devil because Jean-Marie crossed himself before and after he passed the fellow. When asked, Jean-Marie replied he had just been blessing the hour. Marie told him to not make a show of his devotion and to avoid anything that drew attention to his piety. Her advice was that in everything, simplicity and modesty is best. It was counsel he took.

THE HARDSHIP OF LIFE DURING TIMES OF WAR

The Vianneys lived during troubled times; it was the Age of the Enlightenment and the Reign of Terror for all good Catholics in France. War swirled near them as Lyon resisted and then fell to the Revolutionary forces. The churches remained closed since priests had to take an oath of allegiance to the Republic in order to function. The true church went underground and a few priests, disguised as carpenters or laborers, remained in their districts to minister to the faithful. The punishment for hiding a priest was deportation, and large rewards were offered for turning in anyone who helped them. All statues, crucifixes, pictures, any kind of religious object had to be hidden. For the crime of saying evening prayers one could be arrested and imprisoned. Revolutionaries had destroyed the wayside shrines. All evidence of the Christ and his church were to be wiped out.

Mass was held secretly in homes or barns in the dead of night. Often the Vianneys had to walk miles in silence and stealth in order to attend. Jean-Marie was eager to go, but the others complained. Marie was one of those irritating women who hold up one child for the other's example. "Can you not be like Jean-Marie, who is always the keenest of all?"

Jean-Marie's first confession was delayed until he was eleven. First Communion preparation and the celebration likewise had to be carried out in complete secrecy. Every evening they risked betrayal when they invited the beggars to pray with them after the meal. All these dangers were resolutely undertaken by the whole family as no more than their duty.

Because of the political situation, the children had hardly any schooling. The local school closed, and other efforts were makeshift. Besides, Jean-Marie was growing older. By the time the national picture changed and the church and Catholic schools were allowed to open again, his father needed him to work on the farm.

Jean-Marie wanted to be a priest, but he was almost seventeen years old with the education of a ten-year-old. He had no Latin, which was necessary to enter seminary. He finally confided his longing to his mother who hugged him to her heart and cried happily. His father was another story.

Under his mother's advice he broached the subject as they rested after a hard day's work. Matthieu, good Catholic though he was, would not hear of it. Catherine had just gotten married and the dowry had been paid. The elder François had been drafted into the army and Matthieu had paid a substitute to take his place. There was no money for an education for Jean-Marie. Besides, he was too old, and he was needed on the farm. He wouldn't even be able to catch up with his studies. It was hopeless. Jean-Marie remained silent, but his mother did not.

She argued with her husband, but she only succeeded in

making Matthieu more set in his ways. The battle went on for two years until a priest opened a small school in the nearby town of Ecully. Marie was quick to point out the advantages: Jean-Marie would be close, it wouldn't be expensive, and he could lodge at her sister's house. He could even come home and help on weekends. Matthieu gave in and Jean-Marie, almost nineteen years old, went to school.

Not for long, however. He was conscripted into the army in 1809. At first his father refused to try to find a substitute. At last, moved by Marie's tears and his son's grief, he tried but was unsuccessful.

Jean-Marie was forced to report to training, but quickly became very ill and was put in the hospital. Marie begged the nursing sisters to be allowed to take care of her son, but she was not allowed. He stayed there for six weeks, and upon release he was ordered to rejoin the army in the rearguard. Along the way, running a fever and exhausted, he ended up following a deserter and—as if by happenstance—deserting the army as well. He hid for over a year in an area that harbored many such deserters.

At one point the good widow for whom he worked, Madame Fayot, went for medical treatment near Lyons. She arranged to stay at the Vianney home. Jean-Marie sent with her a letter full of "sorrow and repentance." Marie was thrilled to hear from her son and wept with joy. She had been grieving for her son and had recently visited his old teacher, M. Balley. "Do not worry about your son, Mother," he said to her. "He is neither dead nor sick. He will never be a soldier, for he is destined to be a priest." This comforted her greatly.

Matthieu Vianney was not pleased to see Madame Fayot or to hear from his son. The family had been fined severely because of Jean-Marie's desertion. Gendarmes (the police) had even been quartered on the property as a punishment until their son turned himself in.

At the end of the year, a general amnesty was declared to

celebrate the wedding of Napoleon to the Archduchess Marie-Louise. Jean-Marie was now free to return home if he could find a substitute. His younger brother, Cadet, would have been conscripted at any rate, so he volunteered to go in his brother's place. Nothing has been recorded about how much pressure, direct or indirect, his mother may have put on her youngest son.

Jean-Marie returned home only to find his mother deathly ill. She had only hung on to life to see her son safely home again. Overjoyed, she held him long in her arms. She gave him one last present, a white alb made of high-quality lawn with painstakingly intricate embroidery over the lower part. It was just the right length.

She had looked out for her son, believing in him and helping him until the end to do what she believed was the will of God. On her deathbed, she extracted a promise from her husband not to stand in the way of Jean-Marie's quest for priesthood. It was a promise he was glad to keep. On February 8, 1811, two weeks after her son came home, she died where her children had been born: in the same bed, under the same picture of the Blessed Virgin.

All Jean's life her memory was fresh and vibrant to him. He could not think of her without tears of gratitude and love. He once confessed to the Comtesse de Garets that after his mother died all attachment to the world died as well. He became a priest and is now the patron saint of priests.

Jean-Marie, by his own admission, owed much to his mother and to his father as well. Like St. Thérèse of Lisieux, his sanctity arose from within the family where it was nurtured and thrived.

Marie was just a peasant, just a mother, just a wife. She did nothing extraordinary to foster the vocation she must have sensed her son had. She was just faithful to her Catholic faith, although it was a dangerous time. Her methods were similar to many things we do naturally, without thinking about it. To talk of God, to turn her children's minds and hearts to "the good God," as her son was so fond of saying, must have been as natural as breathing. Her relationship with God and faith in him, then, must have been more natural still.

Marie lavished the same loving care on her other children, though they responded in varying degrees. She was first a mother, not only the mother of a saint. We can learn from her this simple humility and ease in sharing our relationship with Christ and love for the church with our children. Who knows? We, too, might one day be a mother of a saint.

⚘ FOR YOUR LIFE ⚘

- Marie consecrated her children to the Virgin Mary before they were born.

- She tried to secure the first and last waking thoughts of her children for God.

- Marie led them to a love for the Virgin Mary early in life.

- They were taught to love prayer by her own example of a vibrant prayer life.

- She took the time to explain the Mass over and over to the young children.

- Marie recognized her son's call and did everything she could to foster it and help him on his way.

"I Was Born to Have Children"
Zélie Martin

There is no guarantee that we will live long enough to finish mothering our children. Zélie Martin died when Thérèse was four years old, but her mothering lived on through her two oldest daughters.

ZÉLIE MARTIN WAS FORTY YEARS OLD, "... the time when one is a grandmother." She realized that her child-bearing years were virtually over, yet she wanted another baby. Many women would dread a mid-life child, but Zélie was afraid she might not be able to conceive. "I love children to the point of folly. I was born to have them. . . ." Just before her forty-second birthday, she gave birth to a daughter on January 2, 1873, after half an hour of labor. This last rose from the autumn of her life is known to history as "The Little Flower," St. Thérèse of Lisieux.

Zélie was momentarily "surprised," as she wrote, that the baby was not a boy. Her disappointment passed quickly, and within days she was writing, "She smiles already. She looked at me attentively, and then gave me a delightful smile."[1]

This was the same woman who wept fifteen years earlier after her wedding on the morning of July 13, 1858, because she would never be a nun. How did such a dramatic transformation take place? Through her love for God that transcended any specific vocation, she learned that marriage was the way God would make her holy. "I want to be a saint," she wrote to her sister. "It will not be easy, for there is much wood to be pruned and it is as hard as flint."

Zélie desired God's will more than anything else in her life. If he had called her to marriage, well then, she would embrace the vocation with all the intense energy and ability within her power.

Zélie's childhood had been an unloving one. Her father was not a bad man, but he was domineering and dour. Her mother, though she was fond of her daughters Marie-Louise and Zélie, was overly harsh, rigid, and rarely affectionate. She obviously preferred her son Isidore to them. "My childhood and youth," Zélie later wrote to her brother, "were shrouded in sadness; for if our mother spoiled you, to me, as you know, she was too severe. Good as she was, she did not know how to treat me, so that I suffered deeply." It was a mistake she made every effort to avoid with her own children.

Within two years of Louis and Zélie's marriage, Marie-Louise, the first of their nine children, was born. During the next four years three more daughters, Marie-Pauline, Marie-Léonie and Marie-Hélène joined their sister.

Zélie thoroughly enjoyed being a mother and loved being able to nurse the first three, but when Hélène was born she found that her milk was insufficient. A wet nurse had to be found for the baby. This was the first of the separations from her infants Zélie had to endure because of nursing problems.

She no longer had any regrets about her vocation, and her joy in marriage knew no bounds. Even when she had to walk miles to the home of the wet nurse to visit her baby, her love only deepened. "I cannot believe I have the honor to be the mother of such a delightful little creature. Oh indeed, I do not repent of having married."

Life in Alençon was comfortable but not luxurious for the Martin family. They lived in a modest house with a small garden. Louis had his own business as a watchmaker and jeweler. Zélie, proficient at making the famous Point d'Alençon lace, had begun her own business at the age of twenty-two. She employed up to twenty workers who would make the lace according to the desired pattern. Zélie would then collect these small pieces of lace, intricately join them together, and then would sell them to the fashion houses of France.

In 1870 Louis sold his business to take over the management and financial affairs of his wife's work. Together the Martins made the business very profitable. Because their work was centered in the home, both Louis and Zélie were able to spend much of their work time in the midst of the children.

Every morning they went to Mass at six as a couple, though Zélie admitted that some sermons bored her and she listened only because she knew she should. She belonged to the Third Order of St. Francis and was active in one or two other church societies.

They had a deep love for the Virgin Mary and passed it on to their children. A large shrine to Our Lady was decorated every May in their home. Zélie repeatedly noted the answers to prayer she had obtained through Mary. She was very practical and unpretentious in her approach to God.

The Martins kept the fasts and abstinences of the church, and Zélie found them trying at times. Louis was stricter in his observance and sometimes embarrassed his wife when he would not bend the rules for visitors. "How I long for Easter!" she would sigh during Lent.

GOD'S GRACE AT WORK IN ZÉLIE

In the spring of 1865, shortly after the birth of Hélène, Zélie noticed that she was never without some discomfort in her breast. That pain was a cancer that ravaged her entire body and finally killed her twelve years later. She was not worried about it. "I had said to God, 'You know that I have no time to be ill.' I was heard beyond my hopes and I boasted of it to myself a little. Then he seemed to answer, 'Since you have no time to be ill, perhaps you will have time for much trouble?' And I assure you, I have not been spared."[2]

Though they loved their girls immensely, both parents longed to have a boy. They begged St. Joseph to intercede that they may have a son who would be both a priest and missionary. Soon after Zélie gave birth to Marie-Joseph-Louis, but he died six months later. After further prayers and novenas, they had a second son, Marie-Joseph-Jean-Baptiste, but he died at nine months. Deeply distressed, the Martins did not ask God for another son. These two sorrows were followed by the joy of a healthy little girl, Marie-Céline, who was born in 1869.

Life in the Martin home was crammed with prayer, work, and good times. Though the Martins did not entertain many guests, other than an occasional priest or relatives, many people came through their house during the week. Once a week the girls who worked for Zélie brought their work. On another day clients would come. On Thursdays they served the poor and sick who came to their house or else the Martins would visit them in their homes.

The work of finishing the lace was never-ending. Often Zélie would have to get up early and work late in order to complete an order when there was sickness in the house. Zélie loved her work and yet, like all of us, sometimes complained about it: "This lace will be the death of me!"

All was not work for the family. Every day the family

would pray in common. Sundays were days of rest when the family would go on walks together. Zélie would write long letters to the two oldest daughters boarding at the Visitation school in Le Mans and to her brother and his wife, Isidore and Céline Guérin.

Neither Louis nor Zélie believed in stifling gaiety for the sake of piety. Alençon was the scene of three large festivals a year, of which the Martins went to at least one. There were pilgrimages and holidays at the seaside or at their cousins' in Lisieux where there would be rides in the country, parties, and festivities to the great delight of the children. Zélie and the girls would make fritters, a deep fried pastry, for feast days, and evenings would find them playing checkers with Louis or reading together.

Their lifestyle may sound quiet and boring in comparison to the frenetic pace of our world. To them, however, it was full, rich, and satisfying. Louis and Zélie disdained frivolity, it is true, but not enjoyment itself. Rather, the Martin family took their greatest pleasure in one another's company.

Shortly after Céline's birth, five-year-old Hélène died in her mother's arms from what seemed to be a cold. This death affected Zélie much more than the other children's did. Two sons, her parents, and her father-in-law had passed away within such a short space of time that she had little capacity to handle another death. Hélène was the third of their children to die, and perhaps Zélie feared that all her children would follow one after another.

Each of these deaths tried Zélie's faith. Each death was a challenge to grow in trust or to wither in bitterness. Both Louis and Zélie wept openly at their children's deaths, but somehow they were able to confide their sorrows to God and turn to him in their intense grief. By faith they were able to grasp a difficult and painful truth: because it was God's will it was to be borne with patience and trust.

From these trials, Zélie emerged with a firm grasp on the reality of eternal life. She had no illusions that the world could offer lasting happiness or satisfaction. If there was one thing that life had taught her it was that death was always near. Above all, despite all, there was the good God and the promise of heaven. Every sorrow of this life made that clearer to her.

Such a frank and almost brutal appraisal of life did not make her grim and austere; rather, her faith in God and love for him grew. Grace was at work, and she responded beautifully. She was energetic, cheerful, compassionate, and a shrewd businesswoman quite willing to make good use of the world's desire for finery.

After the death of Hélène, Zélie's sister, a Visitation nun, wrote a prophetic letter to her: "One day your unshakeable trust in God will be splendidly recompensed. You can be very sure that he will bless you. . . . Wouldn't you feel you had a rich reward if God, so well pleased with you, gave you a child who would become that great saint you have so longed for?"

GOD ACCEPTS ZÉLIE'S SACRIFICE

"So well pleased with you . . . "is a precious insight into the splendor of Zélie Martin's life. Thérèse would be the final affirmation of her mothering. She would not live to see her become a saint, but Thérèse's sanctity would be a sign of God's pleasure in Zélie's faithfulness and life of sacrifice. Others, with the advantage of historical hindsight, have recognized this truth. A pilgrim to Lisieux penciled in these telling words on Louis and Zélie's grave, "Thank-you, dear Christian parents, for giving us a saint to look after us."

This great reward was still far in the future. Between Thérèse's birth and Zélie's death much suffering still lay ahead for the Martin family.

In 1870 Marie-Mélanie-Thérèse was born. Unfortunately, her wet nurse ignored the child, and Mélanie grew deathly ill. Frantically, Zélie hunted for someone to take her place, but before another woman could be found the baby died. She never expected to get over this last death and feared that she would never have another child again. However, there was not much time to grieve.

The Franco-Prussian War swept into their quiet small-town lives and caught them up into world events as the Prussian army marched upon Alençon. Nine soldiers were billeted at their home.

Zélie, with her characteristic forthrightness and no-nonsense attitude, did not let them order her about. "I am not putting myself out over them. When they demand too much I tell them that it is impossible."

The war did not last long, and life returned to normal for the family. Zélie's sister-in-law, Céline Guérin, gave birth to a son, Paul, in 1871 but he died immediately. Zélie consoled her by sharing how she had been able to cope with the deaths of her four children:

> I am deeply grieved at the misfortune that has just struck you. Truly, you are sorely tried. It is one of your first troubles, my poor, dear sister. May our Good Lord grant you resignation to His holy will. Your dear little child is with Him. He sees you, he loves you, and you will find him again some day. This is the great comfort I feel and still feel.
>
> When I closed the eyes of my dear children and buried them, I felt the sorrow indeed, but it has always been resigned sorrow. I did not regret the pain and cares I had borne for them. Several people said to me, "It would have been better if you had never had them," but I could not endure this sort of language. I did not think that the sufferings and anxieties could be weighed in the same scale with the eternal happiness of my children.... It was especially at the death of the first that I was most vividly aware of the happiness of having a child in Heaven. For

God showed me in a sensible manner that He accepted my sacrifice. Through my first little angel, I obtained a very extraordinary grace.[3]

The grace she mentions was the healing of Hélène from one of her illnesses. This daughter later died, but for Zélie it took nothing away from the fact God had healed her on an earlier occasion.

Marie was thirteen, Pauline twelve, Léonie ten, and Céline was almost four when Thérèse was born. The two older girls were at the Visitation boarding school where their aunt lived.

The lump in Zélie's breast had grown progressively worse, but she did not go to the doctor. At that time, operations were not normally performed for such cancers. Thérèse's earliest years were her mother's last. Zélie was dying and would have to hand over the care of her youngest children to her oldest daughters. She was forty years old and had been unable to nurse her last four babies, probably because of the tumor. Nor could she nurse Marie-Thérèse-Françoise when she was born in 1872.

Thérèse began to sicken and after a few weeks it seemed as though she, too, would die like her brothers and sister. Zélie wrote, "I often think of mothers who have the joy of nursing their children themselves; and I have to see them all die one after another!" The baby had intestinal problems and restless nights.

Since Thérèse was named Françoise after St. Francis de Sales, Sr. Marie-Dosithée wrote, "You should pray to St. Francis de Sales and promise, if the child should recover, to call her by her second name, Françoise." Zélie was indignant. "Only when the last hope has gone, will I promise to call her Françoise," she exclaimed.

By February the situation became desperate. Louis was out of town on business, and she was alone with her fear.

She wrote to her sister-in-law of one terrible night: "The night seemed long. All the gravest symptoms which preceded the deaths of my other little ones were showing themselves and I was very sad. I set off at daybreak for the nurse, who lives at Semallé, about six miles from Alençon. On the lonely road I met two men who rather frightened me, but I said to myself, 'I should not care if they killed me!' I felt death in my soul."[4]

Rose Taillé was not willing to go, but Zélie was passionate in her appeals and desperate enough so that Rose's heart softened and she agreed to stay in Alençon for a week. Her husband was not quite so agreeable and sent one child after another to order his wife to return home.

As soon as they came into the house, Rose said it was useless because the baby was dying. Zélie rushed to her room and knelt before the statue of St. Joseph to intercede for the life of her daughter. She struggled mightily to resign herself to God's will, even as she begged for life. Rising she went downstairs to find Thérèse nursing hungrily. Suddenly the baby ceased and fell back into Rose's arm as if she died. Fifteen minutes later, Thérèse opened her eyes and smiled. She began to get better from that moment on.

Rose returned to the farm after a week and took little Thérèse with her. "It is very sad to have brought up a child for two months and then be compelled to entrust her to the care of strangers," wrote Zélie. Thérèse lived there for over a year. She could not bear to be parted from her nurse, not even for the length of Mass. Thérèse screamed and screamed until Rose returned to fetch her. How much pain Zélie must have felt to be rejected by her daughter in favor of the wet nurse!

Finally, when she was fifteen months old, Thérèse came home to stay. Zélie was in her element, and her letters to Marie and Pauline at boarding school are bursting with her joy and satisfaction over her youngest daughter.

THE EARLY YEARS OF ST. THÉRÈSE

A beautiful little child with blonde hair and blue eyes, she was dearly loved by everyone in the family. "My first memories are of smiles and the most tender caresses," Thérèse wrote in her autobiography.

She was "full of mischief," her mother wrote. Thérèse, as well, remembers that she was far from perfect: "Céline seems naturally good.... But I can't be too sure how the little minx will turn out, for she's such a little madcap. She is more intelligent than Céline, but nothing like as gentle and she is stubborn beyond words. It's quite impossible to budge her when she says no. . . . Yet she has a heart of gold, is very affectionate and without a trace of shyness."[5]

Thérèse often pushed Céline and hit her. She was sassy at times. She also tended to be somewhat vain about her looks and clothes. Thérèse tells us of one incident where she was being dressed for a party and was a bit peeved that she could not go sleeveless. ". . . I thought I should have been much prettier with bare arms."

Zélie loved to dress up her girls and do their hair but in simple and subdued styles. She taught her children to laugh at fashion by pointing out how quickly it changes and how little it had to do with eternal life with Jesus.

One day Thérèse could not get into a room so she lay down and blocked the door. Her mother told her to get up. The next day she did it again. "You hurt little Jesus very much when you do that," she was told. Thérèse did not do it again. To please Jesus was held up as the reason to do or not do anything. Accustomed to loving God from their earliest days, their hearts were tender enough to be guided by such gentle means. Sensitivity to her faults enabled Thérèse's mother to teach her the art of self-denial and self-mastery.

It was Zélie who taught her girls to count their sacrifices with disks or some small objects. Marie made chaplets for the girls to encourage them as she herself had been trained as a child. Thérèse's doctrine of the "Little Way" is the supernatural fulfillment of her parents' lifestyle and method.[6]

The children were taught not to whine or look miserable, but to offer up their little sufferings to Jesus. Zélie taught them to do their schoolwork or chores, even if they had a minor illness. This lesson was modeled by Zélie as they saw her continue to take care of them while in excruciating pain.

Zélie would only be able to mother this future saint for four short years before she died. When they were merely seventeen and fifteen, Marie and Pauline took over the mothering of Céline and Thérèse. It is only logical to assume that their methods were drawn primarily and directly from what they had seen and heard their own mother do as she raised them. To understand how Thérèse was raised we need to look at what Zélie did with the older ones.

Zélie's triumph lay in her ability to mother her first children in such a way that they could mother her last ones as she would have done. Her principles, values, and attitudes were faithfully transmitted to the two younger children. All the girls inherited her simple and straight-forward approach to God. Zélie's letters resound with forthrightness and insistence on the transience of the world. These qualities all characterized her daughters as well.

Zélie's letters are delightful. Her personality comes across in vivid, glowing colors: loving, devout, but not smooth and easy. She says disconcerting things that seem too human for the mother of a saint. "Oh dear! how tired I am of suffering! I have not a grain of courage left. I am impatient with everybody." "... I often say during the day: 'My God, how I long to be a saint!' and then I do not labor to become one!"[7] She calls her daughters "little pickles" and says she has had enough after three days of being alone with them and wants some peace and quiet. In other words, she sounds like someone we might know.

The family lives for us through her letters. She chats about daily happenings, and we feel as if we know them. Thérèse's talent for writing is reminiscent of her mother's charming talent of observation and flair for words and analogies.

Zélie's discipline never relaxed for a minute. If something was wrong, it was always wrong and not overlooked one time and severely punished the next. It was a tradition Marie and Pauline kept up with the younger children. Thérèse appreciated this when she was older. "I wonder how you managed to bring me up so affectionately without spoiling me, for you never overlooked a single defect. You never scolded me without a reason, but neither did you, as I very well knew, ever go back upon anything once it had been settled."[8]

At fifteen Marie came home to learn to sew and help with the house. She went to dances and to house-parties with more wealthy friends. Sr. Marie-Dosithée wrote to warn Zélie about the foolishness of letting Marie go on this way. Zélie wrote in exasperation to Pauline, "Are we supposed to shut ourselves up in a convent? When living in the world, one cannot behave like a savage. Besides I quite like the idea of Marie having some entertainment. It will help to cure her of her shyness. One mustn't accept everything my sister says, saintly woman though she is."

But privately Zélie did have her concerns. Zélie, who had stayed decidedly away from all worldly activities, was somewhat uneasy about her daughter associating with the very rich. When Marie began to lose interest in religion and devotions, Zélie was upset. She convinced Marie to go on a retreat for a week. Marie was just as blasé when she came home. Zélie did not let matters rest. Two retreats later, Marie came to herself and began to change.

Zélie breathed a sigh of relief and wrote to Pauline, "I am quite satisfied with Marie. The things of this world do not penetrate her as deeply as do spiritual things. She is becoming very pious. I think that she will be a religious. I would like her to be a saint."

Pauline was still at school and her mother's favorite, her "easy" child. Céline was at home with Mama. Léonie was the difficult one. She was slow at school and would still need to be tutored at twenty-two. Unattractive, always sickly, she was the "middle child" and felt separated from her sisters. Corrections, reproofs, and discipline had no effect on her. Her mother wrote about her:

. . . [she is] a model of insubordination, having never obeyed me save when forced to do so. In a spirit of contradiction she would do precisely the contrary of what I wished, even when she would have wished to do the thing asked of her. In short she obeyed only the maid.

I had tried by every means in my power to win her. Everything had failed up to this day, and it was the greatest sorrow I have ever had in my life. . . .

As soon as she is with companions, she seems to lose control of herself and you never saw anything like her unruliness. Well, I have no longer any hope of changing her nature save by a miracle. It is true that I do not deserve a miracle but I am hoping against all hope. The more difficult she seems, the more I am persuaded that God will not let her remain like this. I will pray so hard he will grant my petition.[9]

Life went on much as it had, except that Zélie knew she was dying, and the family knew it as well. She kept up a brave front and tried to act even more bustling and cheerful than ever, but she wrote: ". . . I am very far from being under any illusions and I can scarcely sleep at night when I think of the future. All the same I am doing my best to be resigned, though I was far from expecting such a trial. . . . If He thought that I was very necessary to this earth, certainly He would not allow me to have this disease, for I have so often prayed that He might not take me from this world so long as I was necessary to my children."[10]

CERTAINTY OF DEATH CHANGES OUR CHILD-REARING PRIORITIES

She must have mothered with a purpose even more than ever, realizing that she had to train a successor. Her one concern was to provide, both materially and spiritually, for her family what was necessary for them. They still needed a mother; who could fill her role? Her first thought after learning she was dying was to take care of this need. She wrote to her sister-in-law: "Marie is now grown up; her character is of a very serious cast and she has none of the illusions of youth. I am sure that when I am no longer here she will make a good mistress of the home, and do her utmost to bring up her little sisters and set a good example. Pauline also is charming, but Marie has more experience. Besides, she has much authority over her little sisters."[11]

Sr. Marie-Dosithée was also dying (from tuberculosis) and Zélie was preoccupied by it. She visited her one last time and told her that once she was in heaven, she must go to the "Blessed Margaret Mary and say to her: 'Why did you cure her miraculously [of chronic whooping cough as a child]? It would have been better to let her die; you are bound in conscience to remedy this evil.' " Her sister had been the one to whom Zélie opened her heart most deeply; she called her the soul of her soul. "We talk to each other of a mysterious, angelic world, above the mire of this earth." Zélie's condition deteriorated rapidly after her sister died. That vital concourse about heavenly things was necessary to her very being, and when it was gone she began to fail.

On the surface everything seemed the same: Zélie continued to work, keeping the fasts and abstinences of the church, praying the rosary every night on her knees and caring for her husband and family. She kept up her vigorous letters and participated in her family's lively activities. She thought about selling the business but didn't. There were prior commitments to fulfill.

The cancer spread, swellings appeared on her neck, and her pain intensified. Her one regret was leaving Léonie, not Thérèse. She confided her worries about her problem child to Marie: "That is not your father's role, good as he is. Who will love her like a mother?" But even as her physical sufferings increased, the sorrow of her heart decreased. Léonie was changing. Zélie wrote to Pauline: "Since your aunt died, I have implored her to win the heart of this child for me, and on Sunday morning I was heard. I now have it as completely as I could have wished. She will no longer leave me for a moment, kisses me until she nearly stifles me, does anything I bid her without question, and works beside me all the day long."[12]

Marie had discovered that the maid, Louise, domineered the child through a system of terrorism to obey no one but her. This had been done so secretively that not even Zélie was aware of it.

Louise had been with them for many years and seemed to be entirely trustworthy. Her original desire was to help with this impossible child, and she did have a sincere love for the family. Louise did not cause the problem, but she greatly exacerbated it by usurping authority and tyrannizing the child.

Perhaps it is difficult to understand how such a thing could happen under the watchful eyes of two very committed parents. There was no reason not to trust Louise, officious though she was, with any of the children. Why should they be suspicious? Many parents today who have suddenly discovered that their children have been sexually abused by a close friend or relative of the family can empathize with Zélie's feeling of betrayal and anger.

Zélie reacted in justified hurt and dismissed Louise immediately. "I no longer wished to have her in my sight." Her Christian mercy moderated her anger, and she allowed her to remain for a little while, though she was not permitted to speak to Léonie at all.

Zélie embarked on a gentle system of treatment to help

Léonie change. Transformation of her character continued to take a long time. Marie would later write to her father, "I am hoping more from the protection of my holy mother than from my own poor efforts, to complete from on high the transformation of my poor sister. . . . I notice that she has been changing daily for some time. . . . I am sure it is our darling mother who is obtaining this grace for us. . . ."[13]

Louis, a great believer in pilgrimages, convinced Zélie to go to Lourdes. She never liked being away from home, and only her great love for him made her decide to go with the three older children. The trip was a disaster. Zélie was very upset when Marie lost Sr. Marie Dosithée's rosary. Lack of sleep, a mix-up about hotel reservations, bad food: the litany of mishaps goes on and on. Though she immersed herself in the baths four times, she felt no relief. On the contrary, she fell and twisted her neck so badly it hurt her until she died.

The girls kept pestering her every hour to see if she had been cured. The whole journey was a continual final penance for her. Her daughters were disappointed, and when she returned she had to answer hundreds of questions from believers and bear the taunts of skeptics.

"I am not sorry I went to Lourdes," she wrote to her brother, "although the fatigue has made me worse; at least I will have nothing to reproach myself with, if I am not cured. In the meantime let us hope."

By this time the pain was excruciating. She could not sleep in any position for more than a few minutes. Nothing eased her pain, but she would not let anyone sit up with her at night. "Oh, thou who hast made me," Marie would hear her cry out, "have mercy on me."

The two youngest girls played in the garden quite unaffected by the whole affair. They counted their good deeds on strings of beads that Marie gave them, blew soap bubbles, learned their lessons, and made little altars to the Virgin Mary.

Zélie still insisted on going to Mass every day. ". . . It took courage and extraordinary efforts for her to reach the church," wrote Marie. "Each step she took reverberated in her neck and sometimes she was forced to stop to regain a little strength."

On August 9, 1877 Marie and Pauline arranged to hold "the Visitation of Holy Mary of Alençon," a prize ceremony for the two younger girls' lessons. Zélie wrote one of her last letters about her joy and pride in her two little ones.

After this Céline and Thérèse were often sent out of the house. Zélie asked Louis to take them for a boat ride. During the weekdays they were sent to Mme. Leriche's house. These weeks were graven on Thérèse's mind and heart:

> "Every detail of our mother's illness is still with me," wrote Thérèse in her little memoir written for her sisters, "especially the last weeks spent on earth. Céline and I were like two unhappy little exiles. Every morning a neighbor came for us and we spent the day with her. Once we had not had time to say our prayers before leaving, and on our way Céline ... mentioned it very nervously to this neighbor, who said: 'Well, of course you must say them,' and left us alone together in a large room. Céline looked at me and we said: This is not what Mummy does. She always prayed with us."[14]

It was Zélie who brought Thérèse to understand God's motherly love. "Mama is the atmosphere of love, and, above all, the atmosphere in which one prays. ... Only when their mother is no longer there do they realize that they have always prayed with her: one prays within one's mother as naturally as in the Church. ... How otherwise can a child be trained in prayer, in realizing the invisible presence, except by the sacrament of visible, tangible love?"[15]

Thérèse was deeply impressed by the ceremony of Extreme Unction which she and Céline were allowed to witness. Shortly after midnight on August 28, 1877, just after the Feast of St. Monica, Zélie Martin died. She was not quite forty-seven. Léonie, Pauline, and Marie were awakened in time to be with her, but the two little girls slept on.

One of Thérèse's most vivid memories was the sight of the coffin and her father lifting her up to give her mother one last kiss. "Everyone was so preoccupied that they forgot to explain things to the littlest ones, or perhaps they thought the girls couldn't understand. I don't remember weeping much, and I spoke to no one about how keenly I felt it all."

Thérèse later wrote, "At this time I entered the second period of my life. It was the most unhappy one. . . . The moment Mummy died my happy disposition changed completely. . . ."

Losing one's mother at any age is a wrenching experience, but Thérèse came to see it in light of God's providence: "I had to be refined by trials and had to suffer while still a child so that I could be offered to Jesus as soon as possible. Just as the spring flowers begin to grow beneath the snow and open in the first rays of the sun, so the Little Flower of whose memories I write had to pass through the winter of trials."[16] The language is hers but the resolution, the faith, and the hope hidden behind those words was the legacy of her mother.

None of us has a guarantee that we will live to see our children's children. We can learn from Zélie to fix our eyes on eternal life and raise our children to value union with God more than anything else. Zélie's life invites us to consider how we would change our priorities with our children if we, too, knew we were going to die. What values would we feel we must pass on? From Zélie, we learn that the time to mother our children for heaven is now.

❧ FOR YOUR LIFE ☙

- Zélie was consistent in her disciplining; once a decision was made it was never changed.

- Her children were discouraged from complaining about slight aches and pains.

- She gave them unexpected moments of ease and refreshment from daily routine.

- Full and instantaneous obedience was expected.

- Zélie taught her children to keep count of their good deeds or their sacrifices. She taught them that these were good goals to strive for.

- She prayed with her children daily.

- Louis and Zélie used spiritual means, such as novenas, Masses, prayer, and pilgrimages to seek God's help for their children's health and well-being.

↣ FOUR ↢

Birth in the Flesh and Spirit
St. Monica

Monica risked alienating her son in this world in order to have him by her side in the next.

MONICA WAS A HOLY TERROR in everything that had to do with her son Augustine. She was convinced that he was going to become a Christian and nothing, especially not Augustine, was going to stop her. She was a woman consumed by one desire only, the salvation of her family, and dependent on only one source, God. Monica's story is one of tenacious faith and persevering prayer.

Born in A.D. 332 in a Christian family, Monica lived most of her life in Tagaste, North Africa. Augustine records one marvelous story about her childhood:

The maidservant in charge of the children forbade them to drink any liquid between meals. She thought that this would teach them to drink wine with moderation in their latter years. But Monica had a mind of her own.

Her parents would send Monica to fetch wine from the big barrel in the cellar. At first, she would just sneak a tiny taste before filling the pitcher. Then the taste became a sip, and

63

the sip eventually became a little cup that she would polish off before returning upstairs.

Augustine breaks the narrative to wonder what would have become of his mother if another servant had not caught her in the act. During a spat this woman called Monica a wine-bibber. Monica was stung to the quick, repented, and never stole wine again.

This story is particularly enjoyable because it reminds us of our own childhoods. Who hasn't pilfered something at some time? Which one of us hasn't used such incidents from our lives to teach our own children about right and wrong? Perhaps Monica, who lived sixteen hundred years ago might have a lot in common with us. At least her faults, if nothing else.

We cannot speak of Monica without speaking of her famous son, because everything we know about Monica we learn from Augustine.[1] The way he tells the story he sounds like an only child, but it isn't true. He had at least one brother, Navigius, and at least one sister.

Apparently they must have embraced the faith more readily than their wayward brother. At the very least, Monica certainly did not have to exert herself for their salvation as she did for Augustine.

Her efforts were not without mistakes. Augustine, looking back from the age of forty-three, portrays a woman who grew in character, holiness, and motherhood throughout her life.

She married Patricius when she was about twenty-two years old. He was a Roman citizen and a free man but poor. Violent-tempered, unfaithful, and generous, Patricius was indifferent to spiritual matters. He was content to leave the children's religious upbringing totally to his wife.

Monica took full advantage of his tolerance and taught her children Christian doctrine, though she did not have them baptized.

At that time in church history, baptism was often delayed until just before death. Many people were unsure that they could fulfill the serious responsibilities that baptism carried. Rather than fail to keep their promises, they just didn't make any until the last possible moment.

Monica followed this custom when it came to her children. As soon as they were born, she traced the sign of the cross on them and sprinkled them with blessed salt. This was the customary way of dedicating infants at birth.

As a child, Augustine knew the basics of the faith and mentions that he was accustomed to pray to God. Once, when gravely ill, he begged to be baptized, and Monica almost succumbed, but then the boy recovered and it was deferred.

Augustine writes that she predicted the great waves of temptations he would undergo in his early manhood and chose to delay his baptism. She felt that if he fell into sin he could still be forgiven and begin anew. On the other hand, if he had been baptized and then fallen into grave sin, the damage to his soul would be much more severe. [Note to the reader: This view, which was popular in Monica's time is no longer theologically tenable given the grace baptism accords to resist temptation and given the power of the Sacrament of Reconciliation to absolve the contrite from serious sin.]

She could hardly depend upon Patricius to steer her son clear of the shoals of sexual misconduct. Unfaithful to his own marriage bonds, Patricius would hardly encourage chastity or fidelity in his son.

Augustine writes very little about Monica's practical methods of mothering him when he was a child. It is only when he is a teenager, when many women think their job is almost over and start gearing down, that we see her just getting up to speed. Monica's motherhood was to begin in earnest.

As brilliant as he was, Augustine did not like to study when he was young. Beatings at school were common, and his parents were not sympathetic to his sufferings.

There were few avenues to financial stability and social success for a poor free man in the ancient Roman world, and education was one of the faster ones. Both of his parents were determined that Augustine would become established as an educator himself. Their ambition was all-encompassing and consuming: "pig-headed resolution" is Augustine's description of his father's attitude. No sacrifice was too great for them, and they scrimped and saved to make his education possible.

Monica, for her part, was just as ambitious as her husband, with one added difference. She thought that education, even though it was strictly pagan, would, in time, help Augustine find his Savior.

It was precisely Augustine's intelligence and learning that God would use so powerfully in the future. But Monica did not even suspect this. She had no idea that her son would become one of the leading defenders of the orthodox faith in his own day and one of the most significant theologians ever known. Patricius' and Monica's sacrifice is still paying a rich dividend today.

Sixteen-year-old Augustine had learned to enjoy his studies when they were interrupted for a year due to lack of funds. During this period his time was generally unsupervised, and he had no responsibilities. Left at loose ends, Augustine started hanging around with a gang of boys.

AUGUSTINE AS A YOUNG MAN

He was also experiencing the "brambles of lust" overpowering him and felt there was no one to root them out, certainly not his father. Patricius laughed when he noticed Augustine's puberty and early began anticipating his grandchildren. Monica, on the other hand, was alarmed when she heard of his active virility. She warned him not to commit fornication but, above all, not adultery.

Augustine would have none of it. He thought her counsel was womanish advice that he would have blushed to follow.

Years later he realized God spoke through his mother and that when he rejected her words he was rejecting God's law.

Monica feared for his virginity and sexual purity but did not take practical steps to have Augustine married. Less ambitious seventeen-year-olds often took a wife. Augustine indicates that here Monica erred in judgment. But she thought differently.

She knew Augustine. She knew he would not follow her advice. For her, the greater sin would be adultery; therefore, if he would sin, let him sin freely. She had living proof that the marriage bonds were not an absolute antidote to lust, and so she would not press for an early marriage.

Besides, Augustine recognized that she was "unduly eager" that he excel in his studies, and a wife would be a hindrance to his success. Apparently, she entertained hopes that a rich Christian heiress would marry her son one day and be the instrument of his conversion.

Monica was a hard-headed pragmatist about life in general and her son in particular. She was in the process of becoming a saint; she wasn't one yet. Augustine writes that she had left the center of Babylon but loitered in its outskirts. Her worldly desires for her son's prosperity would have to go, and she would have to learn what God's priorities were. She wasn't a fast learner. This very problem cropped up in Milan when she found and arranged a marriage with the heiress of her dreams. This attempt ended in failure.

Soon after, Patricius died, and Augustine moved to Carthage to pursue his studies. Fascinated by big city life, he began to frequent the games and the theater.

The games, of course, included gladiator contests, brutal man-to-man conflicts usually ending in the death of one of the competitors. Chariot racing, somewhat more dangerous than our stock car racing, was the tamest of the available amusements.

The theater was ribald, explicit, and definitely pagan. Other examples of lewd religious practices were common sights. Africa led the ancient world in eroticism and Carthage, the rest of Africa. Hardly the environment to send a young man impaled on the brambles of lust.

Augustine solved that thorny problem for himself. He began to live with a woman and had a son by her.

Many Christian mothers would object strenuously to any or all of these activities. How Monica felt about these is unknown, but she did kick Augustine out of her house when he returned home.

It is a difficult situation when a grown son comes home with his live-in girlfriend. More than one parent has refused to house them together. However, this was not the reason why Monica shut him out.

He had picked up something in Carthage that disturbed Monica more than an illicit alliance. He had become a Manichean, a member of an outlawed religious group. This development brought about a profound change in Monica's relationship with her son.

Before this point, Augustine had portrayed his mother as ambitious but a peacemaker, gentle and soft-spoken with her husband and in-laws. She was witty and capable in her dealings with others. From then on he depicted an intense, quick-thinking, tenacious adversary to his plans.

Monica had no qualms about standing up to her brainy son and arguing the faith, nose to nose, countering falsehood with truth. Though not formally educated, she knew her faith, and that was enough for her.

Like many modern cults, Manicheism took elements of Christianity and distorted them. It seemed plausible and appealed to the young intellectual's reason.

Manicheism taught that special knowledge and a certain way of life was needed in order to be saved. The Bible was dismissed as full of contradictions. Above all, they found the idea of God being born of a woman and dying on a cross totally repellent. Diet was very important. Meat, eggs, and even fish were to be avoided. Wine was the bile of demons.

Instead, the devout were to eat only fruits, vegetables, and grains.

Similar in many ways to the New Age movement, Manicheism dealt with a whole array of spiritual beings and forces of good and evil. The divine substance was believed to be everywhere—in trees, rocks, water. To take a bath would be to tear the divine substance in water; to work would be to cause Christ pain, so both must be avoided.

Augustine was an enthusiastic disciple and eager to share his newfound religion with anyone he could. At that time, many Christians did not realize the grave differences between Christianity and Manicheism, and many practiced both.

Monica mourned over Augustine as if he had died, and in her opinion he had died spiritually. Fornication, even adultery, could be forgiven, but to deny the truth of the gospel—that was ultimate death. This state of affairs must have exasperated her a great deal.

Over the centuries writers have commented on her apparent disregard for his sins of the flesh and her practical frenzy over his spiritual waywardness. In their way of thinking, all sins are equally reprehensible. But Monica lived with a pagan husband who only converted shortly before his death. She was very familiar with the results of the sins of the flesh. She knew her intellectual son was vulnerable to the esoteric, the mystical, and elite. Fornication, though poisonous, could not penetrate her son too deeply, but intellectual pride could cast him to hell. Her motherly discernment was that this sin could be fatal to her son and thus required drastic measures.

She would not let him live with her and refused to eat at the same table. Augustine comments that she "loathed and shunned the blasphemy" of his error. Apparently there were some heated exchanges.

This impasse went on for an indefinite length of time until Monica had a dream. She saw herself standing on a wooden rule crying and overwhelmed with grief when a shining young man came toward her, smiling and cheerful. He asked her why she mourned, and Monica told him of her son's certain damnation. He told her to have courage and look carefully around her, for where she was, Augustine would be also. When Monica looked she saw her son by her side.

Monica was convinced that this dream was from God and that Augustine would be saved. She opened her house to him once more and told him of the dream.

He had a different interpretation of its meaning. Monica should not despair because one day she would be a Manichean like himself. She immediately rejoined that the youth did not say "Where he is, there you will be; but 'Where you are, there he will be.'" He was impressed by her perception and logic. Her response, even more than the dream, shook him, but not enough. It would be nearly nine more years before that prophetic dream would be fulfilled.

ON THE WAY TO ROME

Soon after this consoling vision, Monica sought out a bishop who had himself been a Manichean at one time. Would he, she pleaded, speak to her son? He refused point-blank. Augustine was unteachable and too full of the novelty of his heresy. Besides, he was a wily debater and had easily outsmarted a number of people in arguments already.

"Leave him alone," he said. "Just pray to God for him. From his own reading, he will discover his mistakes and the depths of his profanity." Monica still wept and beseeched him to meet with Augustine just once. He finally grew impatient and said, "Leave me and go in peace. It cannot be that the son of these tears should be lost."

Monica accepted these words as a message from heaven. She devoted herself to prayer and to dogging her son's steps. Augustine describes her intercession with the image of labor, certainly a protracted one! She is portrayed as weeping in prayer time and time again—tears that Augustine regards with honor.

Meanwhile, Augustine continued to excel as a teacher of rhetoric, the art of oratory. Nowadays we think of rhetoric as somewhat superfluous, but at that time rhetorical expertise was required to be successful in the imperial service.

His ambitions outgrew his little town of Thagaste, and he returned to Carthage where he was appointed Master of Rhetoric. He wrote and published a book and began to move in the highest official circles in Africa. He had achieved the success his parents had desired.

During the next several years his religious fervor cooled. Through further study, discussions with friends outside the cult, and his own continual doubts, Manicheism seemed less probable.

Life, though successful, had soured. He proposed to go to Rome because of the unruliness of his students in Carthage. In Rome, he felt, things would be different.

In hindsight, he came to see that God had guided him. But at the time, he did not perceive it that way. Neither did Monica. "She wept bitterly to see me go and followed me to the water's edge, clinging to me with all her strength in the hope that I would either come home or take her with me....I lied to my mother, and such a mother, and escaped."

She refused to go home without Augustine and spent the night praying at a shrine that he would not leave. At the same time, unbeknownst to her, he had secretly sailed. In the morning she was wild with grief and upbraided the absent Augustine for his deceit and cruelty, crying out to God all the more in her suffering.

All her prayers, all her love, everything that she tried to do for Augustine was swept away by the wind that blew her son from her. Had God abandoned her? Didn't he care? Were all the visions, words, and prayers in vain? She had begged God to prevent this very thing, but he had not.

Writes Augustine, "You did not do as she asked you then. Instead, in the depth of your wisdom, you granted the wish that was closest to her heart. You did with me what she had always asked you to do." For it was in Rome that he ceased being a Manichean. God did not forewarn her that Augustine was drawing near to salvation; circumstances led her to think he was farther away than ever.

Augustine writes that God had another purpose for separating him from his mother. Her love for him was great, perhaps too great, and definitely too jealous. She wanted to be with him and have him with her. Separation was the greatest punishment of all. Her love became a "scourge of sorrow," in Augustine's words, and the way that God purified her. God would grant her prayer, but first she must learn detachment.

She went home, and Augustine went to Rome. Once settled there Augustine became deathly ill. Monica, though hurt and angry, had never ceased begging God for his conversion. Unknowingly, her prayers obtained God's mercy, and her son was spared. But mercy on whom?

"I cannot see how she could ever have recovered," Augustine wrote, "if I had died in that condition, for my death would have pierced the very heart of her love. And what would have become of all the fervent prayers which she offered so often and without fail? . . . Could you deny your help to her, when it was by your grace that she was what she was, or despise her tears, when she asked not for gold or silver or any fleeting short-lived favor, but that the soul of her son might be saved? Never would you have done this, O Lord. No, you were there to hear her prayer and do all, in due order, as you had determined it was to be done."

Yes, Augustine would become, in God's plan, one of the greatest saints in the church, but that was not why God spared his life. It was for Monica's sake; because of her mother's heart, her faithfulness, her love of God, and trust in his Word to her that Augustine was healed.

Augustine soon tired of Rome. When a teacher's position opened up in Milan, he eagerly took it. He met Ambrose, the bishop of that city and a man who would one day, like Augustine, be regarded as a saint and doctor of the church.

Ambrose was known for his goodness and his powerful style of preaching. A professional speaker himself, Augustine went to church to listen to the man. Augustine was attracted by his kindly welcome. He delighted in Ambrose's charming delivery and at first paid little attention to what was actually being said. Over time he found, however, that he could not keep the two apart. He began seriously to consider Christianity.

FINALLY, ALL HER PRAYERS ARE ANSWERED

Monica, chastened but undefeated, arrived in Milan. Journeys were fraught with danger and difficulty and were not undertaken lightly in those days. In her early fifties, Monica had to leave behind the only world she knew and face a dubious welcome from her son. Besides these hazards, Monica still had one great fear: to die and be buried far from home. She had often spoken of her desire to be buried beside her husband Patricius.

In addition to these hardships, the voyage itself was troubled by storms. When the ship was in danger, she encouraged the crew. She could afford to be confident of their safety. She knew God would bring her safely to shore.

Augustine greeted her with the news that he was no longer a Manichean, but she surprised him because she did not rejoice. She felt that he was in greater danger than ever because Augustine despaired of finding the truth. Despair was worse than delusion.

Monica informed him that God had promised that she would see him a faithful Catholic before she died, and that's when she would rejoice. At least that is how she responded in front of him. In prayer, before God, she hammered on the gates of heaven all the more urgently.

Ambrose was God's angel, she thought, because of the influence he had in her son's life. He thought equally highly of her. Whenever they met, he congratulated Augustine on having such an excellent mother.

Renouncing Manicheism did not mean Augustine was ready to become a Christian. The more he gave up hope of finding the truth, the more ambition consumed him. Monica still believed that worldly success and fervent faith could be bedfellows. Between the two of them plans were made for a advantageous marriage.

As the only surviving parent, Monica, as custom dictated, sought out a suitable girl and made the arrangements. Augustine's faithful mistress was sent back to Africa.

He truly loved her, and she him. This nameless woman vowed to know no other man for the rest of her life. His conduct strikes us as cruel and Monica comes across as a domineering and ambitious mother. Why didn't he marry her?

First of all, if they were to become Christians, neither he nor she could be baptized until the alliance was ended. Second, though foreign to our morality, Augustine was under no obligation to marry his mistress. This fact of life would have been clearly understood by both the parties from the start of the relationship.

A suitable heiress was found, but the marriage had to be delayed two years until the bride was old enough. Was this Monica's clever effort to give her son more time to convert?

Augustine still struggled. He fought his growing convictions, fought against lust, grew more and more restless with his life. Monica merely waited and prayed and took care of Adeodatus, Augustine's son.

Finally, nine years after she believed in faith that he would be saved, Augustine surrendered his life to Christ Jesus and decided to become a Catholic. Monica played no active role in his actual conversion experience. She was not even there. True to form, she did not take it quietly. "She rejoiced. She triumphed," her son wrote.

Monica, Augustine, Adeodatus, and Navigus—Augustine's quiet brother—spent the summer in preparation for Augustine's and Adeodatus' baptism, for Augustine's son had become a catechumen as well. Friends joined them, and long discussions were held. Augustine began to write books from his Christian perspective. The time was idyllic.

A new Monica emerged. All her cares and anxieties were finally laid to rest. She was at peace. For the first time since Augustine was a child, she saw him at peace. Monica became softer, warmer, and gentler. She was in her element. Surrounded by her beloved children and grandson, she happily took charge of them all. A mother until the end of her life, she kept an eye on Augustine's health and cared for all of their needs.

Augustine no longer saw her as his divine adversary, but began to see her wisdom and beauty of faith. This haughty intellectual could finally appreciate her natural, pithy understanding of life and of the faith. His love for her blossomed into admiration as well.

They returned to Milan for his baptism, and shortly afterward Monica, Navigus, and Adeodatus prepared to sail back to Africa. On the way they stopped at Ostia for a rest.

Standing by a window that overlooked a garden, Augustine and Monica shared a mystical experience that surpassed all earthly relationships. They were no longer mother and son or even friends, but two souls wrapped in love of God. They talked of heaven and seemed to have been given a foretaste of it.

Returning to themselves, Monica stated that she was ready to die. She felt that her purpose in life had been fulfilled. "There was one reason, and one alone, why I wished to remain alive a little longer in this life, and that was to see you a Catholic Christian before I died. God has granted my wish and more besides, for I now see you as his servant. . . . What is left for me to do in this world?''

Five days later she came down with a fever. She slipped into a coma and regained consciousness to find her sons standing at her bedside. Augustine tried hard to hold back his tears, and Navigus said that he hoped for her sake she would die in her own country.

Monica had given this last fear to the Lord. "It does not matter where you bury my body. Do not let that worry you! All I ask of you is that, wherever you may be, you should remember me at the altar of the Lord.'' She died shortly after and was buried in Ostia. She was fifty-three years old.

Monica was mother to Augustine in the flesh, but she gave spiritual birth to him in her heart. He was a man beloved by many. His life was encircled by friends, his mistress, and his family. But Monica had a God-given role in his life that he came to esteem only after her death.

Her love for him was total, but she risked alienating him forever if it would help him find salvation. To this end she was willing to look foolish. This great love was honored by God. He honored her by answering her prayers. Through it all, God worked on her, honing her and polishing her until she was truly a saint.

✧ FOR YOUR LIFE ✦

- Monica used her intimate knowledge of Augustine's personality weaknesses and strengths as a basis for decisions and guidance in caring for her son.

- Monica valued her son's salvation over anything else.

- She spent hours in prayer specifically for this intention.

- She did not give up, even when it seemed as if God had let her down.

The Mother of a Nation
St. Margaret of Scotland

Margaret lavished her motherly love and care on her children and her country. Her early life and training prepared her to civilize a rough and rustic nation and help bring it to maturity as a political force in Europe.

T HE STORY OF St. Margaret of Scotland has all the makings of a romance novel or television miniseries. A lovely, intelligent, and cultured princess is shipwrecked on the shores of wildly beautiful Scotland. Then the king, a rough-hewn and commanding man, falls madly in love with her. She becomes queen and uses her power to remake the future of Scotland. As she dies, clutching the cross, her second son arrives breathless from the battlefield with tragic news: her husband and eldest son have been betrayed and killed. Unlike a novel or movie, however, her story is true.

Margaret was born in Hungary in 1047, the daughter of the English prince-in-exile Edward and Agatha, the niece or daughter (ancient histories often get muddled about things like this) of St. Stephen of Hungary. Her father had been forced to flee England as a child after his family lost power.

From childhood, Margaret was exposed to the loveliness of cultured life in Hungary. Because Hungary was on a major trade route, she was familiar with exotic spices, silks, and metals from the East and the use that skilled craftsmen made of these treasures. The court life of Hungary was already developing a sophistication in manner and dress that typified the royalty of the Middle Ages. Surrounded by beauty in worship, court, and home life, Margaret developed that womanly sense of making a house a home that would help her immeasurably later in life.

When Margaret was about ten years old, her father's uncle, Edward the Confessor, became king, and it was now safe for Edward, her father, to return to England. Margaret's family left Hungary forever. Edward died of illness when they arrived, and the family had to adjust to life in a country they had never known and yet belonged to by right of birth. Their homesickness must have been overwhelming, yet they stayed because Edgar, Margaret's brother, was heir apparent to the throne unless King Edward had children.

Life was kindly and civilized in England for Princess Agatha and her children. Edward the Confessor was a very holy man and would be canonized a hundred years after his death. The great Westminster Abbey was just beginning to be rebuilt and is a potent symbol of the piety that flourished at court. Whether Edward the Confessor directly influenced Margaret's love of God is unknown, but his influence over the life at court was far-reaching in fashion and modesty, among other things. Certainly his example would not be lost on a devout princess.

All three children were raised at their holy uncle's court. Margaret had to learn French as well as English, for both were spoken at court. She became proficient at the fine art of needlework, a special technique of solid gold embroidery called *Opus Anglicum*, or English work, used for church vestments. Both the girls were under the strict tutelage of the Mistress of Maidens, a sort of court governess. Margaret learned Latin and read Cassian—a monk and spiritual writer of the fifth century—and the writings of St. Augustine. Margaret had already begun to love and eagerly read the holy Scriptures. She is believed to have been one of the most learned women of her time. And it was probably at the court of Edward the Confessor that she first met her future husband Malcolm.

He had been sent to England for safety, after his father Duncan had been murdered by the Macbeth immortalized six hundred years later by Shakespeare. In the play, Malcolm appears considerably more civilized than he was in real life. Later Malcolm returned to Scotland and defeated Macbeth in battle and became King of Scotland.

After King Edward died, William the Conqueror invaded and subdued England at the Battle of Hastings in 1066. Edgar, Margaret's brother, was not a courageous man and was incapable of fighting for the throne. Always cautious, he offered half-hearted homage to King William and then fled by sea with his mother and sisters. Their ten-year stay in England was over.

SHIPWRECKED IN SCOTLAND

A violent storm wrecked their ship on the Scottish coast, and they came to shore in a little bay known soon after as St. Margaret's Hope. The castaways were rescued by King Malcolm and his men and brought to Dunfermline.

The king's residence was quite a change from the English court for the refugees. At that time, it was little better than a rough hunting lodge and offered little in the way of comfort.

There were no lovely tapestries to shut out drafts or soften the harsh stone walls. Meals were a slapdash affair with the men coming and going or carrying on business regardless of whether the king and his royal guests were finished eating. The king's men were uncouth in manner and speech and knew nothing of the customs of the English court. The womenfolk were good-hearted but unaccustomed to anything except their simple life in the wilds.

How Margaret must have suffered from homesickness that first autumn and winter in Scotland. How alien the Gaelic tongue must have sounded to her ears. An articulate woman in French, Hungarian, and English, she must have been frustrated as she attempted to communicate in a strange tongue. Even the landscape of pine forests and rocky hills, the wail of the bagpipe, and the manner of dress would have jarred her cultured sensibilities.

The widowed king quickly fell in love with the princess and asked her to marry him. She preferred the idea of religious life and declined. Malcolm was an aggressive and powerful lord and was used to getting his way. Shrewdly assessing her brother's character, he convinced the vacillating Edgar of the benefits of cooperating with one's host. Edgar promptly urged Margaret to choose marriage over the cloister.

It was a great day for Scotland when Margaret became its queen and mother. Whether persuaded or constrained to marry, Margaret never regretted her decision. Her vocation was God's gift to her, and she gave herself happily in return.[1] They were married in 1070 at Dunfermline. Margaret's first royal act was to order a church built in honor of their wedding.

To understand the magnitude of her influence as a mother, some knowledge of history is necessary.

Scotland was a land of four warring kingdoms united only by the gossamer strand of overall sovereignty. Pictland, Dalrinda, Strathclyde, and the Angles each held sway over their portion of land. Each had fought and succumbed to the ravaging invasions of Saxons and Danes in the past. Kings had fought to unite the land, but there was no established order of succession to the throne. After their death bloody wars erupted again.

The monastery island of Iona, a bastion of Christianity and

civilization for Scotland for hundreds of years, had finally been abandoned and left desolate. The church had become isolated from the rest of Christendom and was no longer a major transforming force for good. Scotland's internal growth and development had been delayed and stunted by continual conflict. Poverty was widespread. A powerful force was needed to break this destructive cycle.

Malcolm was just the man to forge this diverse people into one kingdom. Known as *Cranmore*, meaning "large head," he was a commanding figure. A cunning warrior, he won the respect and allegiance of the various chieftains. His real gift was leadership combined with innate authority, persuasion, and vision. From his time in England, he realized how civilization and education would advance his people, even though he was illiterate himself.

Gentle and dainty Margaret hardly seemed to be the right woman for a bloody, wild country and king. Still Malcolm not only loved her but realized that she had invaluable gifts and skills that Scotland desperately needed. The greatest of these gifts were her deep love of God and the holiness of her life.

On the other hand, Malcolm must have appeared crass and rude compared to the elegant nobles she had met in England. She was about twenty years old and he about forty. He had a fiery temper as well and, by all accounts, was not exactly a pious man. The earliest biography is silent about this as well as her feelings and struggles in those first years. It is certain that she grew to love him tenderly, however.

The first biography was written at her daughter's request by Margaret's friend and confessor, the Bishop of Turgot. This early account paints her in such glowing terms that it can be hard for us to relate to her as a mother. Margaret made him rebuke her for unrighteousness in her actions or words, but she thought he shirked his duty. Apparently she found faults with herself, but the good bishop has only discreetly hinted at what they could be.

THE FAMILY PRIORITY IS CHARACTER FORMATION

In time, they had six boys and two girls. Very little was recorded about the practical details of their family life. What we do know is illuminating, however, both of Margaret herself and how our children can grow closer to God.

The children were raised to love God above any earthly prestige or power. Three of her sons would reign as King of Scotland and one of her daughters would be Queen of England. They would have to carry themselves with authority and confidence as they lived their lives in the public eye. Yet she wanted them to be as pure and simple as if they were in the cloister.

Somehow she had to accomplish two seemingly incompatible goals: to be in the world and not of it. However, she had in her late uncle, Edward the Confessor, a pattern on which to base her plans. In God's providence she had lived with, and learned from, a devout king who knew how to govern in holiness of heart.

Margaret used a variety of means to achieve this. Her first concern was character formation. Scoldings and spankings were doled out for naughty behavior. Even as children her boys and girls often had better manners than many of their elders. They were polite and respectful to each other. The younger let the older child precede him at Mass or other social functions. They were affectionate and able to get along with one another. Margaret taught them how to behave and then expected them to do so.

As busy as she was, she made a special point of teaching them frequently about Christ and their religion. Margaret brought lofty concepts down to their level so they could easily understand.

Margaret's insistence on this education in virtue paid a royal dividend. She is credited with producing perhaps the best two hundred years of Scottish kings. Three of her sons ruled, successively followed by two of her grandchildren and then two great-grandchildren. The purity of life of all three of her sons was unparalleled. David, her youngest, is called St. David by popular custom.

Only one of her sons, Eadmund, rejected his upbringing and became, for a time, quite ambitious and bloodthirsty. He soon came to his senses, repented, renounced the world, and retired to a Cluniac monastery. Matilda became a good and wise queen. Mary married Eustace, Count of Boulogne, and her daughter became the Queen of England as the wife of King Stephen. Her children had a significant role to play in the history of Scotland and England. Margaret's mothering would affect thousands of other people. How important it is that she stressed a virtuous foundation for their lives!

Her concern for their character formation was the natural outflow of her prayer for them. She interceded with tears day and night that they might love God with all their hearts. Margaret prayed that they would confess Jesus as Lord and worship him. She trusted that their worship would lead to a true love of God. It was only through loving him, she believed, that they would attain the glory of heaven.

Worship was a lesson they had ample opportunity to learn from their mother. She would rise early to pray, read Scripture, and attend Mass. She turned to the Bible as the source of guidance and wisdom, even when hard pressed by her other duties.

Her principle aims for her children were summarized by an old monk of Douay: "Rather to die a thousand deaths than to commit one mortal sin. To give sovereign honor and absolute adoration to the Most Holy Trinity. To abhor all obscene language and uncleanness. To converse with persons of blameless lives and to follow their judgments and counsels. To be firm, constant and unchangeable in maintaining the Catholic faith."[2] She insisted on the necessity of public worship as well.

Religious instruction was not her only concern, however. Malcolm entrusted her with all the education of the children. She arranged to procure the best in books and tutors for them. Keeping a watchful eye on their studies, Margaret made it clear what subjects and ideas she wanted to have taught. One gets the feeling that she had a very forceful personality and used her royal prerogative quite readily.

Her efforts were successful: throughout their lives her children had a strong and far-reaching influence in art, architecture, and literature because of their early training.

MOTHER TO THE NATION

Though this is all we know of how she raised her children, we can guess at her influence by seeing what she did with her "larger family." In fact, it is accurate to say that she was equally mother to the nation as to her own children.

Eight was not enough for Margaret. Anxious about the large numbers of orphans, she began gathering them into homes. Not content to leave it at that, she spent time with nine orphans every morning, feeding them breakfast herself.

The extent of her motherly heart was enormous. No one was beyond her nurturing influence. She and her ladies would make clothes for the poor. Margaret started a free ferry across the river because she noticed the troubles of pilgrims. When she heard of English slaves being cruelly treated, she ransomed them. In order to make it easier for poor people to approach her, she would sit on a large stone in the middle of a field to hear their problems and arrange for aid.

Margaret could easily seem to be one of those terribly efficient, versatile, but exhausting people to be around. Her energy was boundless, her organizational skills amazing. The average mother would not even want to hear how much she managed to pray during the day. Our efforts would seem so paltry in comparison. Yet she wasn't without fault, nor did she seem a superwoman to her contemporaries.

At times, her early biographer seems to suggest that she could be rather demanding and used to having things her way. She was strict and scolded others quite severely on occasion. It is only fair to add she scolded others no more severely than she did herself. A good sense of humor, the redeeming quality of many a saint, is not recorded of Margaret. Perhaps Turgot thought it was too trivial a matter to mention, or beneath her royal dignity.

Above all, she was loved: by her husband, her children, the poor, and all those who knew her. Those who are deeply loved have usually loved more deeply still. I think it was her genuine care and concern, her love and accessibility, that overrode any awe in her obvious accomplishments.

Margaret's concern for the well-being of her people led to a more far-reaching crusade. At this period in history, Scotland was almost completely illiterate. Even the monastic schools had fallen into disuse. The king encouraged her to educate the leaders among his people and from there, other classes of society.

She reformed schools by establishing standards and guidelines to improve the quality of instruction. As a result, education and culture were available to a greater number of people.

Clearly Margaret's own love of learning and extensive knowledge bore good fruit for her adopted country. As a young girl, she might have thought that she was preparing to be a good choir nun, but God had something else in mind: the education of a nation.

Because Scotland was demoralized as a society and the kingship was in such a tenuous state, Margaret developed a plan to bolster the sense of dignity and identity that this struggling people needed. Ascetic herself, she knew that a level of comfort and beauty in worship and daily living would boost everyone's morale. She believed that high moral standards were only possible when people have a sense of personal worth and well-being.

King Malcolm had built the castle of Edinburgh to protect the family while he was away. Margaret set about furnishing it in such a way that it would increase the honor and dignity of those at court. She purchased gold and silver vessels for use at table. She instituted the basic elements of the court ceremonial. To keep the nobles from eating and running, a common problem in today's families as well, Margaret invented the practice of the blessing cup. "Won't you stay to drink the blessing with me?" She would ask ever so sweetly. Abashed, the hasty men would stay put until the end of the meal.

Margaret taught noblewomen how to do the exquisite needlework she had learned in England. They spent much of their time sewing vestments and linens for the church, and hangings and cushions for the castle.

In addition, the queen introduced new styles in clothing and furniture as well. Her exposure to lovely things from her early childhood helped her immeasurably. Soon merchants came flocking with fabric, spices, perfumes, and metalwork that had never been seen before in Scotland. She had first choice, of course, and set the norm by picking only the most suitable wares. Some even credit Margaret with the invention of the famous Scottish tartan plaid.

Her womanly art of homemaking, therefore, increased foreign trade as well as brought Scotland out of the backwaters of culture and into the mainstream of Europe. Her efforts, though they dealt with the domestic sphere, perfectly complemented her husband's strong leadership. While he consolidated the kingdom, she civilized it.

Craftsmen and artists in stained glass and precious metals were encouraged to set up shop in Scotland. They, in turn, taught their skills to the Scots. Margaret fostered the production of illuminated manuscripts, in part by eagerly buying books. These efforts boosted the internal economy and provided a new source of employment for the population.

At some point, Margaret had picked up the basics of medicine as well. She taught others the essentials of cleanliness and nutrition, and this increased the well-being of the nation.

Her example was not lost on the other women at court, and this civilizing influence gradually spread down through society. A world of cleanliness, health, personal care, beauty, and comfort opened up an exciting vista of hope and new goals for the Scots. As a result, women in particular began to experience a new sense of self-respect and a healthy dose of pride in their appearance and moral standards.[3]

The Scottish are fiercely loyal to their clan. It is a wonder, then, that this stranger could come in, marry the king, and revamp the lifestyle of the nobility. Innovators, if they are outsiders, are often seen as busybodies and troublemakers, no matter how helpful their suggestions. God's grace must have been at work both in Margaret and in the people. It is to her credit that she could not only improve the quality of life in Scotland, but also be loved and respected for doing it.

Margaret was less than fifty years old when she died. Most of her children were still teenagers. Her spirit and values lived on in them and in their children. Her legacy of love was preparing a nation to take its place as a powerful force in Europe. Her children, in turn, continued her work of civilizing a rough and wild people.

Delicately reared and highly educated, Margaret could have been a snob and shunned the primitive court and conditions that she found in Scotland. She could have concerned herself only with her family and comfort, but she didn't. Instead, she recognized that her upbringing of learning, beauty, and the arts was a gift God had given her to give to others.

Her intimate relationship with God, her love of Scripture

and worship were the foundation of her ability to mother the nation. It was precisely her motherly heart that God used to enable Margaret to see the needs of the nation and to care for them with all the resources at her disposal.

Not many of us are called to be queens or to transform a nation. Even so, there is much we can learn from Margaret of Scotland about what God desires of mothers.

Perhaps we need to surrender our own mothering to God. We may have put limits on how much, how long, or for whom we will care. Perhaps he might want us to look beyond our immediate family to care for the needs of others.

Margaret's concern for the education, well-being, and comfort of her family led naturally to her interest in others. With the exception of her reforming work in the church, everything she did was with the ordinary means still at our own disposal. She decorated her house, saw to the education of her children, made clothes for them and others, tended the ill—things we do every day.

We can view ourselves as having little impact on the world around us because we are just housewives or career women trying to juggle home and work. Nothing could be farther from the truth: our actions, how we keep our homes, our involvement with our children's education, has an effect on those around us. Our scope of influence may not be as large, but God can use us just as effectively.

Margaret's early life prepared her to fulfill her duty as a mother. Our early life, too, is part of God's plan for our mothering. In what ways can our youth be turned to good advantage in our mothering? Even negative experiences—having trouble at school or moving away from a neighborhood—can help us understand our children's problems.

A historian writing in the nineteenth century called Margaret the "mirror of wives, mothers, and queens."[4] In her we can see how the gift of motherhood can be extended to a whole people without neglecting one's own children.

✣ FOR YOUR LIFE ✣

- The Bible was Margaret's primary source of wisdom and guidance, and she turned to it daily, even when she was very busy.

- She discovered ways to state the basics of the faith in language and concepts her children could understand.

- Her priorities for her children were clear: as a mother her essential task was their Christian character formation.

- Margaret used her housewifely gifts and talents to transform the world around her.

SIX

She Brought Forth a Family of Saints

Alice of Montbar

Alice's intelligence and education were exactly the gifts God used to bring forth a family of saints: St. Bernard of Clairvaux, Bl. Guy, Bl. Gerard, Bl. Andrew, Bl. Humbeline, Bl. Bartholomew and Bl. Nivard.

MANY WOMEN HAVE GONE TO COLLEGE, prepared for careers, fallen in love, married, become mothers, and decided to stay home full-time. They wonder why on earth they got their degrees or worked in their fields at all. *The Complete Shakespeare* is only used as a booster seat and they find themselves debating not *Roe* v. *Wade* but *Pampers* v. *Huggies.* "How can an educated mind find happiness in the home?'' they ask. Does a higher education simply make you discontent with your lot in life if you decide to stay home? Or can it make you a better mother and wife? Alice of Montbar found it made her exactly the kind of mother God wanted her to be.

Alice or Aleth was of noble birth and had good parents.

They decided that she was going to be a nun. The year was 1070, and children did not have any say in their vocational choice. They were lucky if their preferences were consulted at all. Alice was raised according to plan. Happily for her, she wanted to be a nun as well. This meant a great deal more schooling than she would have had if she were to be married one day. Latin would have been required to recite the Divine Office, and it was learned by studying the great writers: Cicero and Virgil.

She was one of the most intelligent and well-educated women of her day, very much like St. Margaret of Scotland. Alice was a woman of rare merit: lovely, noble, rich, intelligent, and deeply religious. Those merits were not lost on one of Hugh, the Duke of Burgundy's counselors, Tescelin the Tawny. He decided that he wanted Alice to be his bride. Her father, in a stunning about-face, agreed. He asked his daughter to accept Tescelin's hand in marriage. At that moment, she told her children later, "I felt as though God were taking my heart." She was shocked and cut to the quick.

The first biographer blithely goes on to say that she recognized that it was the will of God for her life. Maybe it was that simple, but it certainly wasn't painless if it felt like her heart was being ripped out. Regardless of how she felt, in the end she was convinced it was God's will. It was a decision she never regretted and one that brought her joy. Alice of Montbar, age fifteen, married and became the Lady of the Manor of Fontaines not far from Dijon, France.

Prepared to be a nun, she found herself in the opposite vocation. Were her training and desire to live a holy life to be wasted? Could God be at work in a situation like this?

Yes, gloriously so. Alice was destined to become the mother of seven children; six of them have been beatified, the seventh, canonized. St. Bernard of Clairvaux, her son, would lead thirty of his kinsmen, including all his brothers, into the monastic life, be largely responsible for the rise of the Cistercian Order throughout Europe, take a leading role in the religious controversies of his day, and after his death be declared a Doctor of the church. Through God's grace she would be the most significant influence on him both in life and in death. Who she was—her training, character, and most of all, her deep love of God—would fashion him into a warrior for God.

Alice was unconventional as a Lady of the Manor, perhaps because she had not been trained to be one. Or, she may have had the strength of character to disregard the prevailing customs of the day because she wanted to live radically for Christ. It is clear that she differed from other women of her class because she thought and prayed about what was right, what was just, what pleased God in her state of life. Her husband trusted her implicitly and gave her free rein to run the house as she thought best.

For one thing, she refused to have a wet nurse for her babies. Nursing them was something she insisted on doing herself. It was her right and her duty, she felt, to care for her children. Alice believed that even babies absorbed far more than milk from their environment and she wanted to keep them in the purest one possible. Though her understanding was primitive and possibly a shade superstitious, modern pychological studies bear this out: infants are far more aware and receptive to outside stimuli than formerly believed.

Another unorthodox practice was her visits to the poor and the sick. At that time aristocrats simply did not do that sort of thing. To actually go among the peasants was considered foolish, not a holy thing to do. She drew scorn and derision from the ladies of her class because she gave herself and not just money, though she gave plenty of that as well. She would go into the poorest homes and bathe the sick, change the beds, clean the house, fix them meals, even put the dishes away. These were the tasks of the lowliest servants. Take-charge types would be insufferable as they played "Lady Bountiful," but Alice had the knack of coming across as if they were doing her a favor by letting her help. Like St. Jeanne-Françoise de Chantal who would live near Dijon five hundred years later, the humble people of the land called her "Mother."

Around her own house she was a nonconformist as well. She was known to help out in the kitchen when needed. Other lordly houses served sumptuous fare and casks of wine as a matter of course. Not Alice. She was a simple meat-and-potatoes type person, and this was not primarily her preference but her decision. She did not want her children to be spoiled or to become delicate eaters. This unpretentious upbringing prepared them for the life of austerity that they would face as Cistercians. She thought most fashions were too affected and ornate, so she went her own way in the matter of dress for herself and her children as well. Alice avoided both extremes and was not terribly unfashionable, nor did she wear the latest in styles.

Tescelin's position as the king's advisor and his prowess as a knight opened up every social door to the couple, but they chose to live a rather quiet life. Prayer, fasting, and vigils were more important than hunting parties and balls. Showing off or acting extravagant was one thing the children knew would draw their mother's wrath. Moderation and self-restraint, even though they were rich, was more Christ-like, and therefore more to be desired.

Education was the last but most significant area where Alice rode roughshod over convention. Book learning was for monks and nuns, not for knights. It would be a black mark on a knight's valour to know more than a little reading, less writing, and maybe some arithmetic. And Tescelin's sons, like their ancestors before them, had to be knights. Alice agreed, except she insisted Bernard was to be a scholar, not a warrior, and all her children were going to know Latin. That was fine with Tescelin.

HER SPIRITUAL INFLUENCE EXTENDS
THROUGHOUT HER CHILDREN'S LIVES

Guido, or Guy was the firstborn. Gerard came next. When each child was born, she immediately held them up in her arms and consecrated them to God. Then, while pregnant with her third child, Alice had a dream that she could not forget. Many women have strange dreams during their pregnancies, but not all of them are prophetic. She dreamt that instead of a child she had a red and white barking dog in her womb. It disturbed her so much that she sought out a holy monk who reassured her.

"Don't worry, it is all right. The child within you will be a watchdog for the church. He will bark mightily against the enemies of the faith. He will be a great preacher and shall heal many of their sins."[1] She believed him and made that interpretation of the dream the basis of how she would raise him.

Alice believed that it was given by the Lord to forewarn her so that she would raise him more carefully. Her child's ability to carry out the work would depend in part on her, on how she mothered him. She would play a significant role in his life. She must have understood then why she had been educated far beyond what she needed as the lady of the manor. In God's plan, her education was not primarily for her own self-fulfillment, but as a treasure to be enjoyed by her and shared with her sons and daughter.

Bernard was born in due course and after him Humbeline, Andrew, Bartholomew, and Nivard. All the children were taught at home. They learned the basics of the faith and reading, writing, and arithmetic. Bernard easily excelled in his studies. She determined that he should know the Bible thoroughly "as was required by the interpretation of the dream and for its fulfillment," even though it was not customary to study it outside a college.

She thought he needed the breadth and depth of an

education only available at a larger school. Bernard was frailer in stature and health than his sturdy brothers, and his physique was not suited to be a knight. This made his father all the more ready to yield to Alice's desire that Bernard be sent away to school. St. Vorles in Châtillon-sur-Saône would be his home for the next thirteen years.

His mother came to visit him frequently, and she was there that first Christmas he was away from Fontaines. On that feast Bernard had a profound experience of the humanity of Christ. They were waiting to go to Matins, at midnight on Christmas Eve, when seven-year-old Bernard fell asleep in his chair. He then dreamed—or perhaps had a vision—of the whole mystery of Bethlehem. The Virgin Mother even let him hold the baby. Then Alice woke him and they went on to church. This grace he experienced as a seven-year-old child became fundamental to his spirituality and theology as an adult. It began a new season in his life and opened up a sweetness in prayer and love for God. It would seem to be no coincidence that his mother was with him at the time.

Bernard loved his mother deeply, but now he was away from her for much of the time. Just when he had been deprived of the one he loved best in this world, he was given a special, anointed vision of the Virgin Mary. From that moment on his love for Mary grew by leaps and bounds. By loving his mother, he learned to love the Mother of God.

Bernard finished his studies at St. Vorles in 1110 and returned to Fontaines undecided about a career. In August of that year Alice stated quietly, calmly, that she was going to die very soon. No one believed her. She was in good health. She was only forty. And no one said anything more about it. At the end of August, they prepared to celebrate the feast of St. Ambrosian, the patron saint of the church of Fontaines. Alice was running a high fever and went to bed. Every year a grand dinner was served to all the local clergy on the feast day, and Alice insisted that preparations go forward as usual. The next morning her fever was down, but she stayed in bed and asked that the priests come and administer the Last Rites after the meal. It was then obvious to all that she was sinking quickly. She asked those gathered around her to say the Litany of the Saints to speed her on the way. Her reponses were heartfelt and moving until the words, "By thy Cross and passion, deliver her, O Lord." Her face grew radiant, she made the sign of the cross, and then died.

Bernard was crushed. It was only then that he realized how much he loved her, how much he depended on her spiritual insight and counsel. He was sunk in grief for months. His sister Humbeline—so much like his mother—drew him out of his depression. He threw himself into worldly amusements and came close to losing his virginity, but credited the prayers of his mother with rescuing him.

That incident made him realize that he must be all for God or all for the world. He decided to go to Citeaux, but his friends and family talked him out of it. He set off to go to a famous school in Germany to become a scholar priest. On the way he was burdened by the thought that he had disobeyed God and displeased his mother. He thought he saw her and heard her sorrowful reproaches wherever he went. At last he stopped at a church and threw himself on the stones in front of the altar. He begged God to have mercy on him and show him where to go. Suddenly, he felt his mother's presence as if she were standing before him, and at that moment he knew peace and joy. He knew he must go to Citeaux and become a Cistercian.

His father and brothers were involved in the Duke of Burgundy's siege of Grancy. Bernard rode straight there and informed them of his decision. His Uncle Gaudry chose to go with him. Bernard invited his brothers as well. Andrew, about sixteen years old, had just been made a knight and dreamed of earthly glory. He was refusing when suddenly he saw his mother, Alice, standing beside Bernard as if encouraging him to join his brother. She smiled at him and he shouted, "My mother—I see her!"

"Yes," Bernard retorted quickly, "and her presence here is a sign that she wants you to come with me." Andrew went. Thirty relatives joined him all together.

Humbeline was left behind. She was astonishingly beautiful and had a lovely voice. Skilled in music, learned in Latin, and the heiress of the entire Fontaine estate, she was quite a catch. As soon as she was married she forgot her mother's example. She became quite fashion conscious and made the mistake of dressing in some of the latest fashions when she went to see her brothers. She thought she was doing them a favor.

Andrew, as porter, went to tell Bernard that she was there and described her pomp and splendor in detail. Bernard was deeply saddened and refused to see her. He wouldn't allow any of the brothers to see her either. He gave Andrew a message from him to her. She was letting the devil use her to draw others astray. Andrew added: "Why bother so much to decorate something destined to rot and be food for worms? Your soul is going to hell." Humbeline was cut to the heart and immediately repented of her vanity. At that, Bernard and the other brothers hurried out to see her. Bernard encouraged her to live according to their mother's example, which she did. Five years later she entered the convent.

It is unlikely that any of us will appear to our children after we die to comfort and guide them. But there is a way that all of us continue to mother our children long after they have left home. How many times do we ourselves think of how our mother did something? How many times do her sayings come to our lips as we mother our own children? The memories our children will have of us will continue to comfort, guide, and correct them long after we are in heaven with Alice of Montbar.

Today we can feel that the need for our own self-fulfillment is pitted against our family's higher interests.

Using our skills and talents outside the home can seem like the only course of action to relieve the tension—even against our better judgment. But God may be calling us to stay home. Like Alice of Montbar, our abilities may find a different avenue for fulfillment than we can now foresee. Discovering what the Lord has in mind could open up new vistas within the home in ways that include our children.

✦ FOR YOUR LIFE ✦

- Alice insisted on nursing her children because she thought it was her right and duty, even if it was against the conventions of her day.

- She used her strong educational background to teach her children at home.

- She chose a simple lifestyle in food, clothing, and entertainment.

...

SEVEN

Victor Over the Past
Barbe Acarie
(Beatified under Marie de l'Incarnation)

We can be afraid to mother our children because of our own troubled childhoods. Barbe Acarie triumphed over her difficult past and became, not a perfect mother, but a loving and humble one.

BARBE AVRILLOT'S MOTHER did not love her very much. Before Barbe, Madame Avrillot had lost every one of her children at birth and never resolved her grief. Barbe, born on February 1, 1566, in Paris, France, had been dedicated to Mary before she was born in order to insure a safe delivery. As part of the promise, Barbe's mother dressed her in white until she was seven years old. Madame Avrillot was overprotective and unaffectionate, probably because she was worried that this child would die, too. Eventually, Barbe had three brothers. But for some reason, she had to be the one who was a model child in every way.

Monsieur Avrillot was a gently pious man, but he was stiff and uncomfortable around his daughter. Barbe was always a little frightened of him when she was young because he seemed so unapproachable.

The house was a dark and gloomy atmosphere for a little

101

girl. She was timid and nervous around everyone and was only herself when she went to visit a Franciscan aunt of hers who lived in the cloister.

It was a relief to Barbe when, at age eleven, she went to study at Longchamps, the convent where her beloved aunt lived. She was happy and merry for the first time in her life. She felt free at last. For three years, until she was fourteen, Barbe flourished under the strict but kindly tutelage of the Franciscans.

Barbe loved the life so much, she informed her mother, that she was going to be a nun. That did not match Madame Avrillot's plans for her daughter at all, and so she snatched Barbe out of the convent and hurried her back home.

Once home, Madame Avrillot showered Barbe with the latest in fashions, amusements, and pleasures. Everything lovely and pleasing was set before her to coax her back into the world, but Barbe simply refused to play along.

She wasn't allowed to live in the convent? Well then, she would make up her own rule of life. It resembled the Longchamps rule as much as possible. This teenager insisted on living like a nun regardless of what her mother said or did. Teenagers can be tenacious when they want their way, and she held out.

Her mother was just as stubborn as Barbe and far more harsh. The girl, she thought, was just being difficult. So she wanted discipline, did she? Well, let her have it in spades.

Her bedroom was left unheated and Barbe was not allowed to warm herself by the fire. She was forced to dress by the open door where it was coldest. She suffered so intensely from the cold that she lost a toe when a case of chilblain turned septic. Her mother gave her the coarsest of food and little of it. Her mother would refuse to see her for days. Then when she allowed Barbe to see her, she would criticize her sharply. On other occasions she gave her the cold silent treatment.

This harsh and punitive treatment went on for a whole

year, until late in the spring of 1582. The next event that history records of Barbe is her betrothal and marriage to Pierre Acarie on August 24, 1582.

Did she marry out of obedience, though she had not been very obedient in the recent past? Did she marry out of resignation to a will stronger than hers? Or simply to get out of the house? Perhaps she married for love?

The earliest biographers painted the scene very melodramatically. The pure young virgin longing for the convent is forced against her inner convictions into a marriage of obedience. Other biographers make a good case for love, or at the very least the beginnings of love, as the reason for the marriage. Teenagers have been known to change their minds rapidly; no one falls in or out of love faster than adolescents. It's possible.

In any case, later events reveal a deep love and joy between the two newlyweds. Barbe was beautiful, so beautiful that she was known as "La Belle Acarie." Well-born, well-dowered, with green eyes, a shapely figure, rosy complexion, brown hair with red highlights, and a charming personality, Barbe was lovely and sociable.

Pierre Acarie, her husband, was one of those people whose personalities fill the room. A king's counselor, he was rich, daring, and deeply involved in the politics of his day. And he loved her. Together they were a brilliant couple moving easily through the highest echelons of French society.

Although Pierre's sense of humor was captivating at times, he could terrorize his family with his violent temper. He found it difficult to be anything less than the center of attention. Pierre could be a tease and was often petulant. Barbe was afraid of displeasing him, and many people thought she was, at times, too accommodating.

He bought her beautiful clothes and she, who had despised them a year before, delighted in them now. They went to parties and picnics and concerts. Life was luxurious and enjoyable, and Barbe reveled in it.

Upon her marriage, Barbe was placed in charge of Pierre's large establishment. At age sixteen she ruled the house and all that happened within it. Pierre's interests lay in external affairs rather than domestic ones. Unlike many young brides placed in such a heady position of power, Barbe handled it quite well. Even her mother-in-law was very satisfied with her.

Children came along quickly: the first born in 1584, then 1585, and 1587. She doted on them and enjoyed motherhood thoroughly. Many women coming from such troubled childhoods would hesitate to have children. Fear of inflicting similar suffering on their children and the absence of positive role models can afflict them to such a degree that they have little joy in motherhood. But Barbe became a victor over her past through God's action in her life.

Marriage, in short, completely changed the young would-be nun. Her deep religious aspirations evaporated. Her devotion disappeared. Instead of prayers preoccupying her pretty head, she discovered the world of romance novels and played the spinet, a type of piano. Pierre and Barbe still told each other their faults and prayed a bit each evening, but Barbe had definitely abandoned the high road of spiritual life and settled down to a tailgate luncheon in the parking lot.

Why did she go into a religious slump when she married? Is married life itself directly opposed to a vibrant relationship with God? No, as Barbe would discover. Her first biographer gives no clue about why she had drifted away from a vibrant relationship with God. Several clues, though, can be drawn from the way she raised her daughters.

From comments she made and cautions she took with them it would seem that she thought her piety ripened too quickly and was never truly a mature fruit. She seemed to think that, in part, the religious sisters, most especially her aunt, heavily influenced her. The person she loved most was a nun; acceptance and comfort lay in that direction. Her mother was demanding and punitive—characteristics that only made a stubborn girl more rebellious. Once opposition on one hand and acceptance on the other had been neutralized by marriage, her spiritual zeal dissipated.

It also would seem that she finally loosened up the tight rein she had kept on herself and allowed herself to enjoy the world. Yet she would make sure that she taught her children temperance and moderation in the world's pleasures, rather than premature renunciation that could lead to eventual excess.

The last contributing factor is a powerful one indeed: she was loved and desired by someone at last, her affectionate husband. The lack of love and emotional starvation she had suffered all her life were finally being countered by the intense love of a man. This physical reality of love can, at times and for a while, make a woman forget the eternally greater but more intangible love of God.

TOO GREEDY IS HE FOR WHOM GOD IS NOT SUFFICIENT

One day Pierre discovered her absorbed in one of the adventures of *Amadis of Gaul*. He forbade her reading such silly and indecent literature and marched off to his priest to get a list of suitable spiritual books for her to read. Incidentally, St. Teresa of Avila's father found her reading books about the same character and responded by sending her to the Augustinian nuns for schooling. Pierre's point was not to discourage her from reading, but to direct it to better topics. He had the books bound in Moroccan hand-tooled leather and placed on her table.

She dutifully picked them up and began to plow her way

through them until she came to one particular sentence in one of the books. *"Trop est avare à qui Dieu ne suffit."* "Too greedy is he for whom God is not sufficient." It struck her with the force of a spiritual hurricane. Her life was irrevocably, instantaneously, and radically affected.

She did not look the same; she walked differently, her voice changed, and she was no longer timid and afraid of everyone. Her husband suspected she had fallen in love with someone else, and she had: Jesus Christ.

For some reason only known to God himself, Barbe immediately attained the grace of contemplative prayer. She often fell into ecstasies, usually at the most awkward moments.

One morning she went into a rapture after receiving Holy Communion and did not return home after Mass. The family was very anxious by evening and finally checked the church to see if anyone had seen her. There she was, still on her knees. When someone shook her shoulder gently, she was startled, looked up, and asked if Mass was over. Another time it happened when she was talking with her mother-in-law. The woman didn't take it as a compliment.

These kinds of experiences troubled the good but prosaic Pierre and his mother. "What is wrong with my daughter?" she would ask her friends. "My satisfaction with her has not lasted long."

Her husband Pierre decided that he, too, would study the spiritual life to keep pace with his wife. After Barbe found his spiritual help was not helpful, he turned against her.

Pierre began to make trouble for her in many small but hurtful ways. He went to the priests of the local parishes and complained about her so-called mystical graces and how they disturbed her duties as a wife. The ladies in town certainly did not carry on like that. These experiences must be a result of a hyperactive imagination or from the devil. The priests believed him.

On one occasion, Pierre hauled the whole household to church to hear a sermon preached specifically against her. After it was over, Barbe laughed and commented, "He must say what he likes, it will blow over."

These three years of doubt and uncertainty when her family turned against her were hard on Barbe. She did not want these ecstasies and often played the spinet to distract herself from thinking about God too much. She would not spend much time alone, since company usually kept the raptures at bay.

Far from disturbing her duties of life, her deeper relationship with God made her a more efficient and effective housekeeper. Father Duval, her earliest biographer and close personal friend, stated that she never allowed her private affairs to suffer from her spiritual interests. According to him, "Order reigned down to the most minute details."

Pierre, at this time, was heavily involved in the affairs of the League. This was a group of French Catholics who sought to keep Henri of Bern, a Protestant, from ascending the throne of France. Imprudent and generous, he gave much money to the cause and also invested in dubious enterprises.

Barbe gave birth to three more children in 1589, 1590, and 1592. During the siege of 1590 when royalist forces reduced Paris to famine, Barbe took care of the wounded at Saint-Gervais hospital and the sick at the Hôtel-Dieu.

Barbe thoroughly gave herself to her children. Though there were servants, it was Barbe who sat up with them when they were sick and Barbe who made sure they said their prayers. It was unusual in that day and age to see a mother of her rank so concerned with the education of her children. When people would comment on that she would toss it off by saying, "It was no more than what was required of a Christian mother."

She told the Ursuline nuns, a teaching order for girls, "Your care of these girls may well contribute to a general reform of morality. Children are more under a mother's care than their father's, and if the mothers have been brought up with the right principles they will pass them on to their children who, even if they afterwards disregard them for a time, will sooner or later come back to them; because first impressions are never entirely effaced."[1] She knew what she was about: motherhood was the primary way to affect future generations.

Her first priority was for their religious instruction. She took this in hand long before they were "school-age." Once a priest spent his homily complaining about parents who did not bother to teach their children their catechism. He asked a rhetorical question, "If I say to a child, Come, my boy, tell me what faith is?" One of Barbe's children, still a toddler in the arms of his grandmother, thought the priest was speaking to him and answered, "Faith is a gift from God."[2] His grandmother hushed him or he would have gone on with the rest of the definition.

She readily joined her children in their games, even when she was "lost in the depths of God," and gave them "spillikins, draughts, and other toys." Spillikins are jack-straws, which is like tiddlywinks, and draughts are checkers.

Her spiritual life was not opposed to full enjoyment and participation in the life of her family. Unique graces were given to her, she believed, in order for her to be fully a wife and mother. "What is the use of all these fine sentiments, these transports of love and elevation of the soul that should unite us to God, since in failing in our obligations we separate ourselves from him?"[3] This teaching is remarkably similar to that espoused by St. Teresa of Avila and by St. Francis de Sales, who later met her and admired her greatly.

Finally, a holy Capuchin friar, Père Bénédict of Canfield,

cleared Barbe of all suspicion. "All comes from God; she must yield herself to the divine working," he concluded of her spirituality.

THE SOVEREIGN RETURNS TO PARIS

Shortly after this, Henri of Bern renounced his Protestantism and was crowned Henri IV, King of France. Those involved in the League did not fare well when their sovereign returned to Paris. Because of the high regard the king had for Barbe, Pierre's sentence was only four years of exile in a monastery within a two-day drive from Paris. Unfortunately, the family finances were in complete ruin, and the family was left in utter poverty. Pierre, in exile, could do nothing about it.

The mansion had to be closed and the children sent to live with various relations. Barbe stayed in Paris to try to clear her husband's name and to restore his fortunes for him.

Though not trained as a lawyer, she would spend most of the night preparing the case, then often stood in lines outside officials' doors all day long in order to speak to them. Insults and affronts were common for this woman entering a man's domain, but she took them calmly. She finally pled the case before the judges and recovered much of the family estate.

Her sanctity had become obvious even to the king, and many people turned to her for advice. She became heavily involved in reforming religious orders in France. With the financial backing of wealthy ladies, she founded the Ursuline sisters in Paris. Under her instigation, the Carmelite reform begun under St. Teresa of Avila was welcomed into France.

Throughout the day, rich and aristocratic men and women and high-ranking religious leaders could be found at

Madame Acarie's. She developed the ability to turn from the most lofty spiritual conversations to attend to the most mundane of household concerns with ease.

FREEDOM TO CHOOSE WITH MATURITY

Her children were fully a part of her life. She felt that childhood should not be cramped, or it would stifle the intellect. If they looked too serious or pious, she scolded them for it. She thought of this type of behavior as premature fruit that drops too early. That she was thinking back on her own adolescent fervor is quite probable.

Honesty was a passion with her as with so many saints. "If you turn the whole house upside down I will gladly forgive you if you own up when asked. But the smallest lie I will not pardon."[4] Along with truthfulness, she trained them to be frank and open with her. They felt free to tell her anything.

She did not believe in spanking children when they were "still in a passion or wished to make excuses." When they had calmed down and God had convicted them of their wrongdoing, she sent them to fetch the rod themselves. They then knelt down and prayed a Hail Mary or Our Father as they were punished. After it was over, they kissed the rod and thanked it for the good it did them. It is a great loss to parenting not to know how she ever managed to get her children to show such amazing docility and repentance in the face of discipline.

This method of discipline may not be the right one for our times, but what is important is to have a plan and carry it out consistently. Consistency was the heart of her success with disciplining.

She knew her children thoroughly. She tactfully proportioned their tasks to their competency and age level, but she was a stickler about humility. Since they were wellborn, they expected the servants to address them as superiors—

"Mademoiselle" or "Monsieur." But Barbe insisted that the servants address them by their Christian names—Marie, Jean, Marguerite. In fact, the servants had orders not to carry out the children's request, unless they spoke humbly and respectfully, saying "Please" and "Thank you." There would be no lording it over others in her house.

Many of her methods would probably not be ours today. If she discovered that her daughters found some particular task especially offensive, she would require them to do it all the more. Marie, the eldest daughter, was more proud and difficult than the others; therefore, she was not called Mademoiselle by the servants until she was seventeen or eighteen. She found it even more repugnant than her sisters to sweep the floor and do other menial tasks. Barbe discovered that Marie waited until no one was home before she swept the stairs in order not to be, in her view, humiliated in front of them. Barbe corrected her in no uncertain terms and made her do it in front of everyone the next time.

Barbe came to realize later in life that some of her actions were harsh and too exacting. On the other hand, she was trying to deal with an area that all children have difficulty with, vanity and pride. During the beatification process for Barbe, Marguerite stated, "She was always anxious to keep me humble, but she did it so charmingly that I never resented the lesson thus given to my love of self. When obliged to punish me, she did it so that it never occurred to me that she was correcting me unreasonably and the correction never made me angry with her."[5]

If only we knew how she did it! Clearly, her deep love of God and constant striving always to speak out of a recollected state of mind had a great deal to do with it.

In 1599 Pierre returned home but was never his former buoyant self. He could not find a new focus and lived in the past. Barbe's efforts to defer to him met with sullenness and resistance. There is no hint that she ever considered giving up her work for the church to assuage his ego. The eminent cardinal and theologians she regularly met with thought that she was too submissive to his every whim.

Her children were growing up in a spiritual hothouse; the most eminent of France's Counter Reformation were frequent guests in their home. Barbe was concerned that they might slide into a religious vocation without discerning it, assuming it must be God's will. Something very near this almost happened to her oldest daughter.

Marie went to the same convent school at Longchamps as her mother had when she was nine. At ten she, like her mother before her, started to talk about being a nun. As did her own mother, Barbe removed her from the school. But here the parallel ends. Barbe felt the child was too young to choose, but Mme. Avrillot had been upset because it was not her plan for her daughter.

Barbe asked the religious who visited the house not to mention the religious life to her daughter. If she had a real vocation, time would reveal it; there was no sense in waking love before its time. Time proved her mother right.

Marie was even more beautiful than her mother and knew it. After returning home she, unlike her mother before her, took great delight in fashion and all the sundry feminine skills of her day: music, art, embroidery. Her foundations were solid: she had a true love of God and commitment to the faith, but she was having enormous fun being young, pretty, and popular. Barbe did not pressure her but kept her within comfortable limits. Occasionally she would reprimand Marie for excess but was cautious not to do it too often. Because Barbe knew her daughter's heart so well, she knew that eventually Marie would settle into a course either toward marriage or the convent. All the girl needed was time, patience, and the right counsel at the right time.

Madame Avrillot had tempted Barbe with the best of the world. When that failed, she had responded to Barbe's determination to follow the religious life at home with anger and harsh treatment to break her stubbornness. Barbe refused to try to trick her own daughter. Barbe had discerned that her daughter craved the romance of religious life, not the actual vocation at that time. Once removed from that atmosphere the desire naturally passed away.

Barbe would not pressure her about her future. The freedom to choose her own vocation and to take the time to do it was unusual in that age. Only after several years of indecision did she suggest to Marie that she take a pilgrimage to Notre Dame de Liesse for the Blessed Mother's intercession and direction. Six months later Marie applied to the Carmelites.

Barbe overcame her past once again. Perhaps it was healing for her to be able to do for her daughter what her mother could not do for her. The freedom to choose, to make mistakes, and to take her time were precious gifts that only a mother could give her child.

The religious life was seen as a higher vocation—that was the philosophy of the times and of nearly all ages of the church. Yet she was concerned with her girl's motives in choosing it.

"My mother always dressed us very *properly*, though avoiding vanity, and she often told us to hold ourselves up. When a lady of our acquaintance seemed surprised at her attention to these points, she replied wisely: 'I bring up my children so that they can follow their vocation in whatever state Providence calls them: if they enter the religious state, *I do not wish any physical defect to serve as a motive for their step*' "[6] (emphasis mine).

SHE KNOWS HER CHILDREN AND THEIR HEARTS

Nicholas, the firstborn, was very much like his father. He caused his mother the most concern of all the children, probably because he *was* so much like Pierre. She gave him, too, the complete freedom to choose his own profession, except that of a soldier. Because they would duel she said, "They are often in a state of sin." She sent him to live with Francis de Sales in order to study law under President Favre, a good and devout man. Pierre went to college, and Nicholas appears to have taken minor orders, then to have left and married. In spite of his mother's protestations, he did become a soldier and lived in Germany.

Nicholas married a good woman, and Barbe's wedding present was a spacious bed hung with red velvet. Hardly a prudish present, this saint must have enjoyed marriage. There was some mysterious trouble later in Nicholas's life, to some extent financial, but possibly extra-marital because Barbe asked for her present back. "Your eldest brother is in great danger for his salvation . . . ," Barbe wrote to her daughters. "She whom we fear is back in France and will bring much harm to this family, if God of his infinite mercy does not turn him from her."[7] He did settle down after that and lived a sedate life.

Pierre became a Jesuit and a scholar. It was he who introduced the cause for her beatification. That is quite a tribute from a son to his mother.

The girls all became excellent Carmelite nuns because they made carefully reasoned decisions and tested their vocations beforehand. Marguerite was even holier than her mother, according to some.

Pierre's health grew worse and worse, and Barbe nursed him until he died in 1612. Shortly after his death, Madame Acarie joined the Carmelites, the order she helped establish in France, as a lowly lay sister. She took the name Marie de l'Incarnation, the name with which she was beatified. The most influential woman in the church in France chose to take the lowliest post in the order and the most menial tasks. Because she was severely persecuted by the prioress in Amiens, the order insisted on moving her to Pontoise. Her daughter, Marie, was the prioress here and not one of the other religious sisters was more submissive or docile to her leadership than her mother.

It was while she was in the convent that she repented to her daughters for her earlier harshness. "I did you much harm, it was very wrong of me." Her victory over her own childhood and negative role model of motherhood was complete. She did not completely escape that tendency to her mother's severity, but Barbe was able to do one thing that her mother could not. She was able to recognize her mistakes and repent to her children for them. They knew her heart, too, and that her intentions were sincere. Love made the difference, love and the grace of God.

I have not been fair in my rendition of this woman. I have purposely skimmed over her achievements outside the home as if they were of little import. She knew virtually every Catholic authority in France and inspired and directed a great many of them, both men and women, lay and religious. She herself was one of the spiritual leaders of her day, yet she wrote nothing, gave no speeches, held no post. Her only title while she lived was mother and wife, yet merely by her personal influence she did great things for God.

Madame Acarie died in 1618 after living in the convent less than five years. She is beatified as a lay sister, but her sanctity was brought to maturity in and through marriage.

As we approach the end of the twentieth century, many women can resonate with Barbe's troubled childhood. In Madame Acarie's life, we can find hope that we, too, can conquer our past. We can raise our children differently and well. Also we can be consoled when we make mistakes, even if, like Barbe, we don't recognize them until later in life. We, too, by the grace of God can repent and ask our children's forgiveness, and God in his mercy will heal them, often before we ask.

❧ FOR YOUR LIFE ☙

- Barbe reflected on her past in order to avoid her mother's mistakes.

- Especially because her children grew up in a spiritually intense atmosphere, Barbe made sure they had plenty of fun to keep a healthy balance in their lives.

- She believed that her mystical graces were given to make her a better mother and wife, not to take her away from her responsibilities.

- She began to teach her children the basics of the faith when they were still preschoolers.

- She was able to repent to her daughters when she realized that she had wronged them.

EIGHT

Serenity in the Storm
Susanna Wesley

She was a woman who underwent trials and overcame them. Her life was one of disaster followed by calamity, yet because of her personal relationship with her Lord, hardship did not defeat her.

HER FATHER COULDN'T REMEMBER whether Susanna was the twenty-fourth or twenty-fifth child in the family. She would end up giving birth to nineteen children herself. Those two facts alone can make many women shudder and quickly turn the page. "Not my sort at all." But Susanna has a great deal more to her than a large family: she had the secret of serenity in the midst of many children. That is something we all, mothers of one or more, desire to know.

This twenty-fourth or twenty-fifth child was born in 1669 or 1670—her father seems to have had no head for numbers. Samuel Annesley was an outspoken dissenting minister, one of those who separated themselves from the Church of England. He and his family had suffered for his act of conscience, losing position, prestige, and financial resources. Yet when Susanna reached the ripe age of thirteen, she analyzed the facts and stances of both denominations and chose the Church of England.

She was considered to be well-educated for a woman in her era, though she did not read Latin or Greek. She did read works of theology in addition to standard educational texts. As a member of a large and busy household, she was necessarily proficient in domestic matters.

Strong character and capability in women was in decline in seventeenth-century England. A constant whirl of amusements preoccupied them rather than moral or intellectual pursuits. Copious amounts of tea, often laced with brandy, served the same function as our *coffee klatches* today. Religion was unfashionable. Church was simply one more place to see and be seen in the latest apparel. Gossip was coarse, abundant, and often too true. Actresses were beginning to appear on the stage. The average high society woman "patronized French milliners, French hairdressers, and Italian opera singers. She loved tall footmen and negro footboys. She doted upon monkeys, paroquets [parakeets], and lap-dogs. She was a perfect critic of old China and Indian trinkets; and could not exist without a raffle or a sale."[1]

Susanna was a sign of contradiction in this society: well-educated, devout, and deeply involved in the care of her family. She was graceful, beautiful, and intelligent, but was unlike either her high- or low-born counterparts. Neither a do-gooder nor a frivolous matron, she had the courage and character to forge her own way.

She fell in love with Samuel Wesley while discussing theology: he explained doctrinal positions and then made a marriage proposal. They were very attracted to one another on spiritual, mental, and physical grounds—very much in love and very unsuited to one another. She remarked to her son John toward the end of her life, "Tis an unhappiness peculiar to our family, that your father and I seldom think alike." They were married in 1689 or 1690.

Their first home was a tiny place in London, and Samuel,

a poet, wrote for a paper published by Susanna's brother-in-law. He held the position of curate in a small parish. Samuel, their first child, was born during this time.

After Samuel's birth, Wesley was appointed vicar of South Ormsby, and they moved to Lincolnshire which was, in the words of Henry VIII, "one of the most brute and beastly [counties] of the whole realm." The salary was fifty pounds per year plus a rectory to live in. Susanna gave birth to "one child additional per annum": Susanna, the first girl, then Emilia a year later. The baby Susanna died the following spring following a long illness. Twins, Annesley and Jedediah, were born in 1694 but lived less than a year. The second Susanna, called Sukey, was born in 1695. Mary, called Molly, in 1696.

Young Samuel was almost five years old before he spoke, though he could certainly cry loud and long enough. Susanna worried a great deal about it, but no amount of prayer seemed to change the situation. Finally one day when she was looking and calling for him all over the house and yard, a new voice she had never heard before answered, "Here I am, Mother." From then on he rarely stopped talking. Like most children, his favorite word was, "Why?" As soon as he could speak, his mother taught him the Lord's Prayer.

The day after his fifth birthday, Susanna taught him how to read. By noon he knew his alphabet. The next day he could recognize all the letters in the first verse of Genesis, chapter one. By May he was reading the entire first chapter. This was Susanna's standard practice for each of her children.

Finances were tight for the Wesleys. But Samuel was an ambitious man and sought a better post. He found one in Epworth at a salary of two hundred pounds a year, with a rectory, fields to farm, and a barn. Strangely enough, instead of easing, their monetary problems began in earnest.

The position itself carried extra taxes and fees; then the

paper that was published by Susanna's brother-in-law folded and that source of income was lost. They had to buy furniture and their barn fell down. Costs piled up, and the Wesleys sunk deeper in debt, never to rise again. Samuel was not good with money matters. He felt it necessary to spend large sums on Bible commentaries and travel expenses in order to get ahead in the world, rather than on things like clothes, food, and furniture. Emilia later wrote of "intolerable want and affliction" and said they were typically in "scandalous want of necessaries." The Wesleys rarely had more than one servant at any time. That sounds like a great extravagance to us but at that time before the advent of major appliances, hired help was a necessity. With that large a family, outside help would have been crucial in any event.

Another baby, Mehetabel, called Hetty, followed in 1697. Another child in 1698; then John, her tenth, in 1699, but he died a few days later. Benjamin, born in 1700, also died shortly after birth. Twins were born in 1771 but did not live long enough to be named. Anne, the fourteenth child, was born in 1702 and lived. Fourteen children in twelve years and only six lived. Not surprisingly, Susanna was forced to spend several months of each pregnancy with total bedrest.

THE ONE RELIABLE SOURCE OF STRENGTH IN TRIBULATION—GOD

Troubles mounted outside the home as well. Samuel was a very outspoken man. He almost seemed to court controversy and was not one to back down from a verbal fight or to take the diplomatic course. The inhabitants of Lincolnshire were noted for their stubbornness, brutality, and disrespect for the king—any king, no matter which one. Samuel was the king's man through and through, which caused his family endless trouble.

King William III caused a separation between Samuel and Susanna as well. She refused to pray for him because she believed that he was an usurper to the throne. Her husband insisted that she say "Amen" to his prayers. When she wouldn't, he stormed out of the house declaring that he would never touch Susanna or share her bed until she begged God's forgiveness and his. He was gone a year when the king died, but Samuel still wouldn't back down. Susanna redoubled her prayers for God's intervention. At last he returned, but things were still tense between them.

Docility was not one of her stronger virtues. The intelligence that could discern what church to belong to and think through solid principles of child-rearing and education was not about to back down for her husband. Stubbornness was surely one thing the Wesleys had in common.

The populace eventually turned against Samuel because of his political views and began to threaten him, his wife, and his children with physical harm. The house was set on fire, and two-thirds of it burned down. Within the year, their flax field was burnt. Three cows and the watchdog were mutilated. Mobs rioted in the street outside their home on several occasions. Their children were threatened and bullied, and their house was broken into.

God was Susanna's one reliable resource in this trying life. She had taken an hour prayer time daily since she was a child, in addition to family prayers and Bible lessons. After her tenth child was born, feeling the need for more strength, hope, and wisdom, she added another hour of prayer every evening and a shorter period at noon.

Many women caught in the overwhelming challenges of early motherhood find it seemingly impossible to find time to pray. Often the more children they have, the less time they feel they can take to pray. Susanna took the opposite tack: her increasing responsibilities demanded more grace, a closer relationship with the Lord, more intercession and thus, more time in prayer. Her ability to undergo and overcome misfortunes that would crush most other people came directly from the graces received from prayer. An extremely practical woman, she realized prayer was essential but also took certain concrete steps that would enable her to care for her family.

Susanna had to learn to cope with a life that was in constant upheaval. It has been said that people have two great fears. One is that things will never get back to normal and the other is that they already have. Tragedy was normal life at the Wesley house. To counter this, to effectively handle the financial hardships, and to deal with the obviously heavy demands of a large family while still undergoing several months of bedrest out of every year, Susanna developed a highly organized system. Years later her famous son John—the second of that name—asked her to set it down in writing. She replied: "It cannot, I think, be of service to anyone to know how I, who have lived such a retired life for so many years, used to employ my time and care in bringing up my children. No one can, without renouncing the world in the most literal sense, observe my method; and there are few, if any, that would entirely devote about twenty years of the prime of life in hopes to save the souls of their children, which they think may be saved without so much ado; for that was my principal intention, however unskillfully and unsuccessfully managed."[2]

Regularity and order were the key elements of her method. Modern child psychologists recommend consistency and a sense of order, too, as a good way of helping people deal with stressful situations. Whether that was her reasoning or whether she made a virtue out of a necessity, it worked. Her home had to run smoothly with or without her being up and about.

Her children were put on a schedule from birth. It does sound rigorous to us in our spontaneous and instant society. However, we fail to appreciate the extreme amount of manual labor and effort it took to carry out even the most mundane tasks. Without a great deal of order a large family would have degenerated into sheer chaos.

The children learned to eat what was put before them without fuss. They also learned, at a year old, to "cry softly," and not to have tantrums. She set aside some time for each child once a week where each was guaranteed time to be alone with her and tell her whatever he or she wanted. She used this time to speak to the individual needs of each that she had noticed during the week. Each child knew his or her day and that he or she would have her undivided attention for at least that hour.

It would seem that she must have been somewhat of a drill sergeant to accomplish this regimen, but there is no indication of excessive yelling or the use of conditional love on her part to achieve her goals. In fact, one example can teach us a lot about her character.

Kezzy was her slow child—it had taken her a day and a half to learn her alphabet. One day Susanna was trying to explain a grammatical rule to her, but Kezzy could not grasp it. Over and over Susanna repeated it carefully and simply. Finally, the girl caught on. Looking up, Susanna saw Samuel watching the whole affair. "I wonder at your patience. You have told that child twenty times that same thing."

"If I had satisfied myself by mentioning it only nineteen times, I should have lost all my labor. It was the twentieth time that crowned it!"[3]

It requires great love and understanding as well as patience to take that much time. The house was run on the strong power of love and peace, not force. John would later remember "the calm serenity with which his mother transacted business, wrote letters, and conversed, surrounded by her thirteen children." She wrote to her son Samuel, "I do not love distance or ceremony: there is more of love and tenderness in the name of mother than in all the complimentary titles in the world."

One of the means she used to run her house smoothly was to have the oldest child take the youngest that could speak and the next oldest the next youngest and so forth for prayer together twice a day. They read a chapter from the Old Testament and some Psalms to their sibling, then went to private prayers before breakfast. Then, at five in the evening, they read a chapter in the New Testament, more Psalms, and prayers. This habit of giving each child some responsibility for another drew them closer together and deepened their love for one another.

THE SEVEN BY-LAWS BRING PEACE

Another important facet was clear communication with the children. A series of seven by-laws, probably drawn up by Susanna, set out what expectations the parents had of the children. Sometimes Susanna has been portrayed as a rigid, harsh disciplinarian, aloof and remote, yet these by-laws reveal a very wise, humane, and understanding mother.

The first dealt with lying. It is interesting to note that other holy mothers heavily stressed honesty and truthfulness as well. Children often lie habitually because they are afraid of punishment, Susanna observed. If the fault was confessed and amends promised, the children were not spanked.

Lying, "pilfering at church or on the Lord's day," disobedience, quarreling, and other such things would most certainly be punished. Children would not be bawled out or punished twice for the same fault. If they mended their way, that fault was not thrown up to them later.

Every act of obedience, especially if it thwarted their own preferences, was to be praised and often rewarded, "depending on the merits of the case." Even if the child had done a poor job but had done it to please or obey, Susanna's principle was to accept the intention or obedience as of more value than the result. The child would be gently directed how to do better in the future.

All the children must have loved the next rule, especially in a large, poor family: another's private property was just that. Not even the smallest thing, "though it were but the value of a farthing, or a pin," could be taken from the owner "without, much less against, his consent." She went on to observe that this rule could not be instilled enough into the minds of children. Because parents do not insist on this with their children "as they ought," injustice in the world at large results.

Another rule is guaranteed to cut down on the tedious refereeing parents are dragged into day after day. If promises were made they were to be kept. Once a gift was given the donor had no more rights over it. The only exception was if it were given on a condition that was not fulfilled; then the donor could get it back.

All the children knew this was the way things worked in their house. There was no indecision or inconsistency. They ran a strict house, there is no doubt, but one where love was lived out and expressed in the rules of the home.

The last by-law was radical for her time: "That no girl be taught to sew till she can read very well." Women read so poorly because they were taught to sew before they were taught to read, Susanna believed. Some of her daughters read Greek and Latin as well as English. Emilia was a headmistress of a school for a number of years.

John Benjamin Wesley was born June 17, 1703. A year later the first Wesley child, Samuel, went off to school at Westminister. Samuel Jr. wanted to be a minister, so the already strained finances were stretched farther to make this sacrifice. Susanna had home schooled them all, beginning with each child as he or she turned five. The main reason was financial; they could not afford public school for all of their children. But even more importantly, as Susanna wrote in her letter to John, she thought that by doing so she could better help them come to a saving knowledge of Christ.

In our unruly age, where independence, personal rights, and self-will are exalted to the heights, Susanna's advice on dealing with children's willfulness seems authoritarian. We must understand that, for almost all of us, words like subjection, conquering the will, and authority, carry an extremely negative connotation. We have inherited certain misunderstandings of these concepts through the philosophers of the Enlightenment. Susanna's goal was not to dominate her children but to help them overcome the natural disability we are all born with: an inherent tendency to rebel. "To inform the understanding is a work of time, and must with children proceed by slow degrees, as they are able to bear it; but subjecting the will is a thing which must be done at once, and the sooner the better; for by neglecting timely correction, they will contract a stubbornness and obstinacy which are hardly ever after conquered, and never without using such severity as would be as painful to me as to the child. In the esteem of the world they pass for kind and indulgent, whom I call cruel parents; who permit their children to get habits which they know must be afterward broken."[4]

Worse, some parents, she goes on to say, even teach their children to do things and later punish them for doing those very things once the behavior becomes a nuisance to them. If a child is taught to master himself and learn to obey and respect his parents, then they can overlook a "great many childish follies and inadvertencies" or correct them mildly. No willful disobedience should be overlooked, however.

Susanna felt very strongly about this subject and spent most of her letter trying to explain it to her son. A willing heart "is the only strong and rational foundation of a religious education, without which both precept and example will be ineffectual." After all, she points out, "religion is nothing else than doing the will of God, not our own. . . ."

POLITICAL UNREST AND PERSONAL TRIALS

Parliament was dissolved by Queen Anne in 1705, thus requiring new elections. Samuel, as usual, declared publicly that he was going to vote for the Tories in a very Whig locality. Susanna had given birth to another son and was extremely worried about her husband and the family safety, so much so that she was unable to nurse the baby and was confined to bed. A neighbor woman was found to wet nurse the boy.

The day before elections, Wesley went to Lincoln and then fled to Gainsborough after being warned by a friend that his life was in danger. Meanwhile, at home in Epworth, a mob gathered under Susanna's windows and fired pistols, shouted, and beat drums until one or two in the morning. The noise kept everyone awake, including the wet nurse. She finally fell into so sound a sleep that she rolled over on the baby and suffocated him. Finding him dead when she awoke, the woman woke the servants and threw the dead baby in their arms; then they all rushed upstairs to wake Susanna. Before she was fully conscious they placed her dead child into her arms. "She composed herself as well as she could," wrote Samuel to Archbishop Sharpe, "and that day got it buried."

The hope of success and financial recovery tantalized but did not materialize. Instead, Samuel was thrown into debtor's prison where he began immediately to minister to the prisoners. Alone once again, Susanna had to rely all the more on God's grace. She sent her rings to prison to help pay for his board while he was being held at Lincoln castle. The Archbishop of York came to see Susanna and asked her if they had ever wanted for bread. No, she replied, but it was so difficult to get and then to pay for it afterward was almost as bad as not having it at all. The following morning a church official brought by a generous donation.

Martha was born in 1706. Then just nineteen months later,

two months premature, Susanna had another boy. He was so feeble that he did not cry or open his eyes for two months. His name was Charles. Samuel meanwhile embarked on what he felt would be his life's work, a *Commentary on the Book of Job*. He spent a large sum of money on *Walton's Polyglott Bible* while his wife and children went in rags. He sincerely thought that this would make them their fortune and repay them for all they had endured.

Two years later, in 1706, Hetty was awakened by a shower of sparks and the smell of smoke. Samuel woke his sick wife and the family. They all rushed downstairs only to find the outside door locked and the keys upstairs. Samuel ran back upstairs to get the keys.

Six months pregnant, Susanna waded through flames up to her knees. She fell to the ground twice as the fire forced her back. She cried out to Christ to save her, and she managed to get out. In the mayhem outside, she could not locate Samuel and realized that six-year-old John was missing as well. His voice was heard from the nursery and his father tried three times to get through the flames, but they were too fierce. A man standing on another's shoulders had just reached the little boy and gotten him out when the roof came crashing in. From this moment on Susanna knew God had a special purpose for this boy's life. John, too, saw himself as "a brand plucked from a burning fire."

Of the expensive Bible only a scrap remained that read, "Go sell all that you have, take up your cross, and follow me." Twenty pounds in gold and silver hidden in Susanna's room had been fused into a solid lump. Susanna was severely burned up to the waist and was put in bed to prevent miscarriage.

Just as a campfire is put out by scattering the logs, so the Wesley family was scattered into different homes for six months after the fire. Emilia stayed with her mother and father, and the other children were dispersed among family and relatives while a new rectory was built. Two months after the fire, Kezziah was born. She was named after one of Job's daughters born to him after his restoration.

While her children were apart from her Susanna wrote them long letters to try to teach and guide them, even though they were separated. Some of these are quite dense theological tracts, considering they were written to children. It was a habit she never lost. She wrote to them since "they might pay more attention to it because it comes from their mother, who is, perhaps, more concerned for their eternal happiness than any one in the world." She encouraged them to save her letters to read when they were older and could understand more. For her, the supreme duty of a parent was "the health, comfort, and support of the children in this world, but more so their immortal soul."

Part of her duty, she believed, was to lay a good foundation so that they may act upon principles and be always able to be satisfied with themselves. She had reasoned out for herself what her principles were and thought they should do the same. "In all things act on principle.... Often put this question to yourself: Why do I do this or that? Why do I pray, read, study or use devotions, etc? By which means you will come to such a steadiness and consistency in your words and actions as becomes a reasonable creature and good Christian."[5]

With no intention to detract from her praiseworthy efforts at childrearing, it is still important to point out that she was not perfect. One weakness in Susanna's otherwise exemplary method was glaringly revealed when the family was together again:

Never were children in better order. Never were children better disposed to piety, or in more subjection to their parents, till that fatal dispersion. . . . In those [families] they were left at full liberty to converse with servants, which before they had always been restrained from; and to run abroad to play with any children, good or bad. They soon learned to neglect a strict observance of the sabbath, and got knowledge of several songs and bad things, which before they had no notion of. That civil behavior, which made them admired when they were at home, by all who saw them, was in a great measure lost; and a clownish accent and many rude ways were learned, which were not reformed without some difficulty.[6]

Like a nervous mother who keeps her children away from everyone else who has the slightest cold or flu, Susanna had protected them from every possible source of moral infection. They were only "germ-free" inside their home environment, however. Once outside the glass bubble, they succumbed to the first bug that came along: disrespect, rudeness, ignorant speech, and crude ditties. Model children by default, not by choice, they never had a chance to own what they were taught. The Wesleys had not inoculated their children against the world, just removed them from it. Guided exposure to other views, values, or ways of life would have helped them make a personal assent to live a highly moral life.

"We entered on a strict reform," wrote Susanna after their new home was finished. Susanna did not allow her children to order the servants about. The servants were directed not to do anything for the children unless the request was polite. The children knew that those were the parents' orders. Bothering the servants when they were eating was not allowed. Swearing, obscenities, crude speech, or rude names were forbidden. School hours were strictly adhered to: they were not permitted to wander off and do other things but were taught to attend to business at hand. Fighting among themselves brought Mother or Father in as an umpire and their decision was final.

The reform was successful and the children had no major lapses once they left the family nest. Indeed, their love and respect for their mother endured for their whole lives.

Wesley traveled to London for extensive lengths of time to represent his diocese. This gave rise to a curious episode where Susanna ended up reading sermons and leading prayers in her kitchen for as many as two hundred people because the curate refused to hold Sunday evening services. Her son John was the first ordained Anglican minister to allow women to preach at Methodist meetings. It would seem that the memory of his mother's kitchen could have strongly influenced his innovation.

Life settled down for the Wesleys. Poverty continued to grind away at them, but no major tragedies occurred. In 1724 Samuel took another pastorate at Wroot, four and a half miles away, in addition to his one in Epworth. He insisted on moving his family from their large and newer house into a ramshackle smaller rectory at Wroot. This way he could rent the Epworth home. Like the rest of Samuel's financial plans this one ended up breaking even at best.

All three of her boys were away at school. Both Samuel and John were able to win financial assistance to further their schooling. All three were ordained priests of the Church of England, like their father. Things were not so happy for the girls. Many of their marriages were not happy. Samuel was difficult and controlling with the girls as they reached marriageable age, and some married in rebellion.

Samuel was thrown out of a wagon and almost killed in 1731. His health continually worsened for the next several years. He hung on, trying to finish the commentary he had started so many years before. Molly, happily married to the curate at Wroot, died with her infant in 1734. By 1735 Samuel was at the point of death. He placed his hand on Charles' head and said, "Be steady. The Christian faith will surely revive in this kingdom; you all see it, though I shall not."

Somewhat later he whispered to Emilia, "Do not be concerned about my death. God will then begin to manifest himself to my family." No one could have guessed how prophetic his remark would be. Susanna had fainted several times at the deathbed; she mourned him deeply even before he had died. Her strength finally gave way entirely, and she was bedridden in a separate room for several days before he passed away.

Amazingly enough, financial affairs stabilized for Susanna after Samuel's death. The income of a thousand pounds was given to her by a relative for her lifetime. She went to live with her daughter Emilia at the school in Gainsborough.

John and Charles had been planning to leave for Georgia in the Colonies but would not go if Susanna needed them to stay. When they laid the matter before her, she replied, "Had I twenty sons, I should rejoice that they were so employed, though I should never see them any more." Courage had become second nature to her by then.

The trip to America was to begin a spiritual upheaval in John's life and consequently spread, like the flames that consumed his childhood, until they engulfed the whole of England in the fire of the Holy Spirit. John preached powerfully and Charles wrote hymns that are still sung in churches throughout the world today. Susanna has been called the "Mother of Methodism" with good reason.

Susanna at first doubted her son's message of personal assurance of salvation. But when she was seventy years of age and John handed her the communion cup with the words. "The blood of our Lord Jesus Christ which was given for thee," she knew in her heart that she was saved. She, who had taught them so very much, had the humility to learn from her sons. "I am become a little child and need constant succor." [Note to the reader: A caution is in order here for Catholic readers. The Catholic church has always taught that no one can know with absolute certainty in this life whether he or she will be saved, except in the rare case that a person receives a special direct revelation from God.]

Shortly after this Samuel Jr. died at age forty-nine. Kezziah died three years later. Out of nineteen children only seven remained alive. In 1742, Susanna died quietly and peacefully, asking her children to sing a psalm when she was gone.

Susanna's life can certainly give us perspective on the problems we face in our daily life. Our problems may be just as tough in their own way—or they may be similar to hers. But we know that a woman not much different from us has "gone the distance." She endured and triumphed over incredible odds, not by herself or on her own resources, but by God's grace found in daily prayer and Scripture.

We, too, can "undergo and overcome" our personal trials with our families through Christ who strengthens us.

↵ FOR YOUR LIFE ↴

- Susanna kept home life as consistent as possible in difficult times.

- The Wesleys had clear standards of behavior that all their children knew and lived by.

- She set aside some personal time with each child weekly.

- She saw good character as the real foundation for good education.

- She praised the children's good intentions or obedience, even when the results were not adequate.

An Intensely Maternal Heart

St. Jeanne-Françoise de Chantal

A mother may be a saint herself, but that does not mean she will not have difficult children who are a challenge to raise.

QUITE A CROWD OF RELATIVES AND FRIENDS gathered to see off Jeanne-Françoise de Chantal as she left her native city of Dijon to begin a new order of nuns. Though not all of them fully approved, the rich and powerful were there to say good-bye. After all, a mother of three young children and guardian of a fortune leaving society to be a nun in a small town was novel at best and at worst, absurd. To be sure, the girls were going with her so she could care for them, and the boy was only a year or two from being presented at court. Still it just wasn't done. Yet they all dearly loved this precious woman, and tears came to their eyes and hers as she slowly moved around the room bidding each *adieu*.

At last, deeply moved with emotion, she came to her son,

Celse-Bénigne. She loved him very much and knew him well. He threw himself at her feet and made a touching speech that almost seemed to be memorized. She responded with words of love and tenderness, and everyone around them wept at this heartbreaking scene between mother and son. He hung on her neck to try to prevent her from leaving. She kissed him and reassured him again. Finally, Madame de Chantal took his arms from around her neck and turned to go into her father's study for a private farewell.

But Celse-Bénigne was not done yet. The teenager, weeping copiously, "managed to drape himself, with unparalleled grace, over the doorstep." "Alas! Mother," he sobbed, "since I cannot detain you, you shall, at least, pass over the body of your son."

Any mother would have broken down in tears, and Madame did. Her son's tutor, as well-acquainted as she was with the boy, chided her, "What! Madame, can the tears of a child shake your resolution?"

"No," she answered, half smiling and half weeping, "but what can I do? I am a mother!" Then she looked up to heaven, as if to draw strength, and stepped over her son's body.

Sounds hard-hearted, doesn't it? But you see, she knew her son: impetuous, talented, proud, reckless, affectionate, a spendthrift, and, above all, dramatic. Both Madame de Chantal and the boy's tutor knew perfectly well that he was simply making a scene and was not above a spot of emotional blackmail.

One can well imagine her real pain of leave-taking, mixed with chagrin and exasperation at her boy's histrionics. A less holy mother would have been tempted to kick him as she stepped over his prostrate body.

Jeanne-Françoise Fréymont was born on January 23, 1572, in Dijon, France. She was, in fact, a descendant of St. Bernard of Clairvaux, the son of Alice of Montbar. She was born into the *noblesse de robe,* those who earned their way into the upper class via the legal profession. Her father, just a magistrate at the time of her birth, was one of the more important chief magistrates by the time she was nine. Her mother died after giving birth to a son, André, nineteen months after Jeanne's birth. She grew up in a deeply religious family and was very close to her older sister Marguerite, as well as to her brother.

Her father personally taught them their religious instruction and "made a pleasant leisure time activity of discussing spiritual matters and even controversies with them," Mother de Chaugy, the saint's first biographer recalled, "according to each child's level of maturity and understanding." Jeanne learned to read and write in French but probably had other subjects. Much of her time was spent learning the indispensable skills of a lady: singing, sewing, etiquette, the popular dances at court, how to read music and to play musical instruments.

After her sister married, Jeanne spent five years living with her and her husband. In this far worldlier atmosphere, skepticism abounded and entertainments were on a lavish scale. Marguerite apparently had no problem adjusting, but Jeanne was unhappy.

Her father could not keep her with him because of his involvement in some political troubles, but Jeanne finally was able to join him in Semur. There she found out that her father had chosen Christophe de Rabutin, Baron of Chantal, to be her husband. Chief Magistrate Fréymont arranged both daughters' marriages to boost the family's social position. Both were marriages into the hereditary aristocracy, the *noblesse d'épée*. Jeanne and Christophe were married December 28, 1592. Though the marriage was arranged for more prosaic reasons, it was a perfect match. They loved each other "madly." She was twenty years old when she became the Baroness de Chantal and mistress of Bourbilly, the Baron's estate.

The management of the house and lands was turned over

to her completely. Her father may have gotten a noble title for his daughter out of the marriage, but his son-in-law got an extremely competent business woman. He needed one; neglected for years, Bourbilly was in terrible financial shape.

Christophe had been somewhat of a playboy before his marriage and may have had at least one illegitimate child. He was no longer a ladies' man, but he wasn't quite ready to settle down to being a land baron. Knights were expected to war on the king's behalf from mid-spring until late fall. Putting Jeanne in charge was not only wise but expedient.

They began married life fifteen thousand gold *écus* in debt. Jeanne was not happy about finding herself holding an empty purse. Nor was she willing to trade her life of leisure and minimal responsibilities for such a heavy load. Christophe resorted to a husband's time-honored motivator: he held up his mother as an example. Jeanne "without further argument, took charge of the business and household management." Whether her education included supervising, accounting, management, and all the other skills needed to run the farms, livestock, and a household is unknown. If she did not have those skills when she married, she learned them fairly quickly.

The outstanding debt was her first priority. To get the farms producing the way they should, changes, widespread and radical, were carried out "gently but firmly." She was so successful at lovingly bringing about a new order of life at Bourbilly that no servant left her service in her whole nine years, except for two she regretfully had to fire.

This latent ability to organize, manage, and delegate served Jeanne in good stead. Little did she know then that she would be totally responsible for managing the fortunes of her children until they were of age and handling all the business of a rapidly expanding order. This experience prepared her for those situations, and she came to value it highly. Writing to her daughter Françoise, she said, "Be sure to apply yourself to managing your household the very best way you know how. If I hadn't the courage to do that myself, we never would have been able to go on living there."

Lovely to behold, lovely to listen to, Jeanne-Françoise was called "the perfect lady," but she wasn't perfect. For her entire life she had difficulty resigning herself to the will of God. Undemonstrative in her affection, she showed it in what she did for others, while neglecting to show her love physically. Jeanne's depth of love was only fully understood by her reaction when her children died or were in difficulty. In her ardent desire for holiness she perhaps expected too much too soon from her children and was definitely too exacting with herself. Her great efficiency and ability to handle many things swiftly sometimes put others off.

Jeanne-Françoise derived a great deal of satisfaction out of her work on the estate. She was overwhelmed by love for her husband, as he was for her. Sorrow had already entered her life: her first two babies died at birth. Finally in 1596 Celse-Bénigne was born and lived. Only women who have suffered the anguish of miscarriages or stillbirths can appreciate the relief and joy she must have felt. Two years later Marie-Aimée was born and a year later, Françoise.

PERSONAL ATTENTION TO THE POOR AND SICK

When Christophe was gone to fight for his country, Jeanne laid aside her beautiful clothes and wore wool or linen garments without ornamentation. She took the opportunity to spend more time serving the poor and devoted herself to the business of the estate.

She attended daily Mass in the chapel and encouraged her servants to do the same. In the evening, the entire household staff would gather for prayers led by Jeanne. She loved to take care of business from horseback. She hung a leather bag from her saddle to hold her Psalter so that she could pray psalms as she rode.

Part of the secret of her success had to be the personal interest she took in the tenant farmers, their families, and her servants. She took the time not only to conduct business, but also to find out how they were and what their needs were.

This kind of personal attention and concern was evident in her care for the poor in her area. We are used to hospitals, clinics, and doctor's offices in almost every town. Medical help may be expensive, but it is usually available. Not so then. Doctors were very few and far between and very expensive. Hospitals were limited to large cities and were overcrowded. The sick and poor in the country had no one but themselves in times of need, unless the lady of the manor extended some kind of help. The difference between Jeanne and other ladies of such position was that she *cared* for the poor. Once again, personal involvement made the difference. They called her "Mother" because she naturally acted like one.

Every evening beggars would enter by one gate, where she would stand and fill their soup bowls, and they would exit by another. Some would slip back into line and go through a second time. When this was pointed out to her she replied, "Do I not present myself at the gate of heaven over and over again, just like these beggars, and does not God look mercifully upon me every time?"

Lest all work and no play make Jeanne seem like a dull sort of saint, the other half of her life must be told. When Christophe was home, she still prayed and cared for the poor, but not as much. Out came the lovely clothes, and she quickly hurried through her chores in order to have time to spend with her husband. Balls and parties were held at Bourbilly, and they went to neighboring chateaus for festivities. It was quite right that she should devote herself to her husband, but, as she so clearly saw in later years, she neglected her God.

In 1601 Christophe was killed by his best friend when a hunting gun accidentally went off. Two weeks later Jeanne gave birth to a healthy little girl and named her Charlotte. The trauma of her husband's death all but destroyed Jeanne. The servants as well as her relatives were concerned because she would not eat and wasted away before them.

The darkness of grief became the light which illuminated the vanity of the world for her. She began to yearn for God with all her heart and to long to consecrate her whole being to him. Daily life with its myriad duties and demands balanced her introspection. Despite her consuming interior trials, she did not neglect her children. Jeanne determined never to marry again, even though her family was opposed to her decision.

ANOTHER CHALLENGE

One year later, her father-in-law, Guy de Rabutin, insisted that she and the children move to Monthelon, his home, to care for him. He was an ornery fellow who had taken one of his servants as a mistress and she had borne him five children. The woman ran his home as if she owned it. If Jeanne didn't move there, the Baron warned her, he would disinherit her children and marry again and the servant girl would, in fact, own it. For the sake of her children, Jeanne died to her own preferences and plunged into her own personal purgatory for over seven years.

The mistress was insolent and patronizing to Jeanne. Madame de Chantal, in turn, repaid her with the burning hot coals of charity. She even went so far as to educate the woman's children for her. Not that this kindness did not exact a tremendous price from Jeanne: pride, patience, love—nothing was left untested. Haughty and domineering by nature, this crucible humbled Jeanne. As painful as these years were for her, it was probably due to this taming of her arrogance that she could successfully lead the Visitation sisters in the future.

After two years of this familial slavery, Jeanne-Françoise met Francis de Sales in Dijon where the bishop was preaching the Lenten series. Within a few months he became her spiritual director and helped her learn to live in her difficult situation victoriously.

He gave her a pattern of spiritual life that he thought should be adequate for a "woman still young, born and reared in aristocracy, the mother of four and occupied with the management of a large fortune." She was to rise at five each morning without disturbing her maid and pray several standard prayers (Our Father, Hail Mary, Come Holy Spirit, Apostle's Creed, etc.). Following this she should meditate on the life and death of Christ or the four last things (death, judgment, heaven, and hell). She should always end with an act of confidence in God. Bishop de Sales thought it should take about an hour.

Afterward she should go to daily Mass and then pray the rosary "recited as devoutly as possible" sometime during the day. Jeanne should not neglect fervent short prayers of praise and adoration, especially on the hour, and spiritual songs—sung devoutly, of course.

Before supper, he advised her, she should take time for an examination of conscience and say five Our Fathers and Hail Marys in honor of the five wounds. "In the evening a full half-hour of spiritual reading. That is quite enough for one day."

"That's great for her but not for me," a modern mom might say. "She had servants, was rich, and could afford to spend all that time praying. I can't because of everything I have to do for my husband and children." We are not obligated to pray as she did, or even as much as she did. Each of us has to determine that with God alone. However, time wasn't the issue for Jeanne. She had as little or as much time as any of us.

From her days at Bourbilly, it is clear that she was a very busy woman. Since her husband's death, she had taken much of her children's personal care upon herself. She got them up at six in the morning, dressed them, brushed their hair, and often did the same for the housemaid-mistress' children. Then she gathered them in a circle around her and prayed with them. She taught them their basic prayers and how to reflect on some aspect of the gospel. Then they all kissed one another and trooped in to say good-morning to their grandfather. Jeanne tried to instill in them respect for older people, especially their relatives. Even the children went to daily Mass. Later in the day she held catechism classes, not only for her children and the mistress' children, but also the poor children in the neighborhood. Francis de Sales approved of her becoming a schoolmistress: "God will be pleased with you for it, for He loves little children: ... the angels of little children love with special love those that train them in the fear of God and instill pious sentiments into their tender soul."[1]

The habit of prayer was second nature to them because they had always been taught to pray from their earliest years. Besides morning prayers and Mass, there was grace before and after meals and prayers before bed. She taught them to examine their consciences, too. They always included a prayer for their father's soul, a prayer to their guardian angels, and closed with, "Into thy hands I commit my spirit." Their mother then blessed them with holy water and stayed with them until they went to sleep.

During the day she took care of the business of running Bourbilly now thirty to forty miles away. Daily visits to the poor and sick were part of her routine. She used them to teach her children to be charitable and compassionate and brought them with her even to deathbeds. This was, as the children saw it, a reward for obedience and industriousness. It was considered to be a great punishment to be left behind. They each had their task: Celse-Bénigne carried the bread,

Marie-Aimée the medicine, and Françoise the money. Charlotte was too young to carry anything.

She tried to teach her children that love of labor was second only to the love of prayer. This is especially noteworthy since they were independently wealthy and did not have to work for a living. In an age where rich women usually led frivolous lives, she saw a purpose in learning to work hard and diligently. Luxury and too much leisure, Jeanne well knew, led to dissipation, selfishness, and vanity. Self-denial, sacrifice, charity, and an ardent love of God are nearly impossible under those conditions. To counteract the prevailing cultural climate they lived in, Madame de Chantal raised her children to keep themselves occupied and busy.

The girls began to sew as soon as they could hold a needle. They hemmed altar linens for churches and made clothes for the poor. "If I wasted my time," Jeanne said, "I should consider it something stolen from the Church and the poor, for whom I am working." It was a philosophy she tried to pass on to her children.

THE "EDUCATION OF THE HEART"

Spiritual yet eminently practical—that was Madame de Chantal to the core. She desired more than anything that her daughters be aware of their "noble and sacred mission" in the world, to be "active and generous Christians, capable of worthily bearing the burden of their vocation."[2] The "education of the heart" was primary, but she did not neglect other aspects of their training. All the talents and skills a girl would need to take her place in society were taught by a governess, and Celse-Bénigne had a tutor.

This "education of the heart" was not only religious, but geared to each child's needs. Jeanne clearly saw their character flaws, and rather than disguising them as virtues or ignoring them, she took on the difficult and usually thankless task of trying to help the children master them.

All the children were physically beautiful like their parents, and they knew it. Vanity was a besetting sin, especially for Françoise. It would appear that Jeanne was not free of it herself by comments Francis de Sales made at some of their first meetings. The nobility were used to spending a great deal of time, energy, and money on fashion. But Jeanne dressed her children simply and the custom of the *grand toilettes* was not allowed. In other words, taking an hour or more to get ready to go somewhere was not acceptable. "She taught them to be earnest, to esteem others for their qualities, not for their dress, and to laugh at those absurd and constantly changing fashions that entail such expense and cause so much sin."[3]

One day she noticed Marie-Aimée was especially proud of her looks so she took her for a walk: "She told her that we ought to blush, since [clothes] are the proof of our lost innocence; that we should recall the stable and the manger in which Jesus Christ was born, the cross upon which He died, and, like the saints, grieve at the necessity of wearing silken robes and golden crowns, since Our Savior wore a crown of thorns."[4]

She reminded Marie-Aimée that St. Bernard of Clairvaux was their relative. If he wouldn't talk to his sister because she was so finely dressed, then Marie-Aimée should not expect her mother to recognize her as her daughter if she did not renounce vanity. These were tough words, but they deeply impressed the girl.

Celse-Bénigne caused her the most concern, however, and was a frequent subject in her letters to de Sales. The boy was gifted but undisciplined and wild; he did not take correction well, was vainglorious and loving but selfish. His grandfather's example was hardly a good one for this headstrong child.

Bishop de Sales suggested that Jeanne inspire Celse-

Bénigne with a "noble and valiant desire to serve God, making small account to him of mere worldly glory.... Do all of this little by little, slowly, gently as the angels do, by pleasing suggestions and without harshness." The angels, according to Francis de Sales, have a "peculiar mixture of kindness, sweetness, firmness, patience, amiability, and holy tact."[5]

Charlotte was gentle and everyone's favorite, and Marie-Aimée, in spite of her vanity, was very much like her mother in character and piety. Françoise was Madame de Chantal's other difficult child. Strong-willed and pleasure-loving and very fond of spending money, she did her best to resist her mother's efforts to moderate these qualities. She shared with her brother a caustic wit and a talent for swift repartée.

Far from forcing her children into a religious vocation, Jeanne considered what they wanted. Celse-Bénigne was determined to be presented at court. Jeanne was full of fear for his well-being, knowing that he was especially prone to the worldly and sexual temptations he would encounter there. Yet, since he was set upon it, she sought the holiest priest she could find to tutor him.

Though the girl was a little younger than customary, Marie-Aimée was betrothed at age nine and married two years later to the Bishop's brother, Bernard the Baron de Thorens. The marriage, however, was not consummated until she was several years older.

THE FOUNDING OF THE VISITATION ORDER

Jeanne's life was about to change drastically. She determined that God was calling her to found an order of nuns under the direction of the bishop. Her father and brother agreed after prayer and discussion but, of course, her father-in-law was not too happy with the decision.

Madame de Chantal would never be able to offer the children a settled home unless she married again, which she refused to do. The life at Monthelon was hardly the best atmosphere to raise either her son or daughters. The order was not intended to be strictly cloistered or particularly austere, and the younger girls would remain with her. Marie-Aimée would be living near Annecy, learning to take over the management of the Château de Thorens, her husband's home. Jeanne would be much closer in Annecy than in Burgundy if she was needed. Celse-Bénigne would be leaving his mother within a year or so, in any case. Even if she stayed, his training would be virtually carried out under the direction of her father and her brother, the Bishop of Bourges. Her time of direct and intense influence was ending whether she stayed or went.

In addition, there was the fact that God called her, Jeanne-Françoise de Chantal, as he does few others, to do a certain work for him. Perhaps this hard-headed businesswoman who was so conscious of her reputation needed to learn to walk by faith and not by sight, so the Lord asked her to do the unexpected and scandalous.

As related, Celse-Bénigne did not take it well. Years later, however, he wrote to his mother: "I wonder at God's providence in our regard. Had you remained in the world, as we desired, had you taken the care to promote our interests that your maternal love and unparalleled prudence would have inspired, you could not have imagined me better settled than I am. God has given me in my marriage every advantage suited to my rank, age, and disposition."[6]

Before Madame de Chantal left for the convent, Charlotte died suddenly from illness. Marie-Aimée stayed with her mother when her husband was out of town, which was fairly often. Françoise stayed with her mother until her marriage. The teenager was not cloistered but went in and out of the convent on visits and to parties. Françoise's love for God cooled as she moved into society. "She was too well received by the world for her not to reciprocate its welcome," Mother de Chaugy wryly observed.

Jeanne's maternal care for her children after she entered the order was so conscientious that she continued to administer their affairs and doubled their income in the span of three years.

Marie-Aimée and Bernard had a very happy marriage that was reminiscent of the love and tenderness between her parents. In 1617, he was ordered to lead his regiment into the Piedmont. Three weeks later he died of illness in Turin. Marie-Aimée was pregnant with their first child. Jeanne had to break the news to her daughter. Exercising all her self-control, she began to talk about abandonment to the will of God and how much he loved her in order to give her courage and resignation. When Marie-Aimée heard the news, she cried and fainted away. Jeanne, at this, fainted away as well.

Her daughter lived at the convent for three months, then suddenly went into premature labor. The labor and delivery was agonizing, and the baby lived only a few minutes. Jeanne delivered the baby, baptized him, and her first grandson died in her arms.

Marie-Aimée lived in terrible pain for a few days. Jeanne forced herself to stay beside her, though her grief burst out violently at times. Her daughter looked tenderly at her and said, "My dear Mother! Oh, I love her more than I can say! Oh, Mother, how I am suffering! Good God! how great are my pains! But what are they compared with the suffering of Jesus upon the cross?" The nineteen-year-old mother and widow asked if she could receive the habit of the order before she died. As soon as she had received the Last Rites and the habit, she was transformed with brightness and died. Francis de Sales closed one eye and her mother the other, then she swooned. He later said of her sorrow, "Nothing was wanting to this grief; it was extreme. Nothing was wanting to this resignation; it was sublime."

Jeanne de Chantal went to extensive efforts to find the best husband for Françoise and wife for her son. She wrote several letters to her daughter that contain excellent advice for any young woman in her first years of marriage. Once again, the practical and spiritual, mundane and sublime are interwoven beautifully as they were in the writer herself. Françoise and the Count de Toulongeon were married in 1620.

Françoise was supremely happy: she was rich, in love, and she moved in the highest ranks of society. Just like her mother, though, her first two children died after premature births. She conceived a third time but was understandably anxious and fearful about the pregnancy. Mother de Chantal was worried as well for her daughter and came to be with her.

Françoise had been sick in bed, but as soon as she heard her mother had arrived she got up and got dressed and went down on her knees before Mother de Chantal. Her friends were convinced Françoise would harm herself, but she was equally convinced her mother was a saint and could obtain from heaven the grace of a safe delivery. Mother de Chantal's heart was deeply touched, and she raised her daughter to her feet. Later, Françoise gave birth to a healthy girl, Gabrielle. Eighteen months later she had a son.

Like many modern mothers, Françoise thought that two were wonderful, but she hesitated about having more children. She dreaded the thought of baby after baby. Still as funloving as ever, she regretted missing the social whirl while she was pregnant. Her main concern, however, was that she wouldn't be able to provide for them "according to their station in life." Mother de Chantal wrote to reassure her:

O God! my dearest child, you are too fond of the things of earth. What do you fear? That the number of your children deprive you of the means of educating and settling them in life according to their birth? Apprehend nothing of the kind, I beg you, for that would be wronging the wise providence of Him who gives them to you, and who is sufficiently good and rich to support them, to provide for them as will be expedient for His honor and their salvation. This is all that we should desire for our children, and not aggrandizement in this miserable and fleeting world.

Courage, then, my very dear daughter! Receive with love and from the hand of God all the little creatures that He gives you. Take very great care of them. Cherish them tenderly, and rear them entirely in the fear of God, and not in vanity.[7]

Her son, meanwhile, was giving his mother much cause for worry. He had a fondness for dueling, which was outlawed by the king. All her letters to the other convents of the Visitation and to the good bishop begged for prayers for both Françoise and her son. She wrote to one of her nephews: "I'm so distressed about him that I don't know which way to turn, except to call on Divine Providence to look after him and [on my part] to turn everything he does over to God, including my own child's health, reputation, and ultimately his salvation as well. . . . I couldn't do anything with him myself if I tried; I cry so much over him that I am blinded by tears, and every bone in my body aches."[8]

Celse-Bénigne's marriage in 1623 to Marie de Coulanges, a good and sweet young woman, helped but did not fully settle him down. Cardinal de Richelieu, the Gray Eminence, deliberately turned the king against Chantal, by telling him that Celse-Bénigne laughed at everyone. He had to leave or be executed. He then enlisted as a volunteer in the army to try to win back the king's favor. His mother wrote to him to encourage him to think of eternity and to keep his soul prepared for death. She also wrote frequently to her pregnant daughter-in-law to keep her spirits up as she worried over her impulsive husband. His faith came to life in 1627 as they approached combat with the English. He received the sacraments and gave his last few days to God. In the first engagement with the British he had three horses killed beneath him and endured twenty-seven pike thrusts. With his last breath he implored God's mercy and died. His mother received the news of his death on her knees, where she wept and prayed for his soul.

In 1633 her daughter-in-law, the widowed Baronesse de Chantal, fell ill and died, leaving a young daughter, Marie or Cantaline as her grandmother nicknamed her. Two weeks later Françoise's husband died, leaving her a widow with two children. At last the lively Françoise was ready to receive her mother's gift of a deep spirituality. She spent the rest of her life much as her mother had: wholly involved in the education of her two children and in prayer.

These years were full of traveling and work for Mother de Chantal as her order grew to over eighty-seven convents. On the way home from one of her trips to Paris, she stopped in Pontoise and venerated the relics of Madame Acarie, already honored as a saint by the people. There is no space here to discuss her "double motherhood," her relationship with her spiritual daughters. She held nothing back in her love and care for them, though. She did not know any other way of being. To love and care, to nurture and guide, was as simple as breathing to her. She was able to found the Visitation Order because her maternal heart formed its bedrock.

AN INTENSELY MATERNAL HEART

Jeanne-Françoise Fréymont de Chantal—wife, mother, widow, and nun—died on December 13, 1641. She was not quite seventy years old. As she lay dying, she requested that they read the account of St. Monica's death.

At last, she truly learned the lesson of total resignation to the will of God. "She asked nothing and refused nothing." She spoke to each sister one by one as they filed by her bed, giving them one last thought to help them. She died holding a crucifix in one hand and a lighted candle in the other, going as one of the wise virgins to meet the Bridegroom.

"Un coeur fort maternel," an intensely maternal heart, describes St. de Chantal perfectly. She loved strongly, passionately, and as long as life itself. Two of her children were "easy." They ran in their mother's footsteps, not without stumbling or mistakes, but were children after their mother's heart. Two of her children were "difficult." They balked and plodded in the way of righteousness. They, too, were children after their mother's heart. She loved them no less than the others. She gave herself all the more to them and for them, to do everything in her power to direct them to God. All of them, easy and challenging, came sooner or later into a right relationship with the Lord.

As mothers we can struggle with our feelings about our difficult children. We can become discouraged over their lack of faith or behavior. St. Jeanne-Françoise de Chantal encourages us, by her life, never to give up, never to stop loving and calling them to righteousness, and never to stop going to the Lord ourselves.

l **FOR YOUR LIFE** m

- Jeanne involved her children in caring for the poor and sick.

- Jeanne made prayer her first priority for the day and taught her children to do the same.

- She taught her children to respect their grandfather, even though he was not easy to get along with.

- Jeanne taught her children that working hard can help one be open to God.

- She praised simplicity and modesty instead of beauty and fashionableness.

- Jeanne continued to call her children to eternal values, even when they were on their own.

TEN

A Mother For Life
Margarita Bosco

Many women approach mothering as a job with a fixed end in sight. When the last child leaves home, they will finally be free to pick up their own life and live it as they please. Margarita Bosco could have done the same but didn't. She chose to mother as long as God asked her to.

D ON BOSCO WAS A MAN OF DREAMS. His ministry had been revealed to him in a dream when he was nine years old. The Lord had often used dreams to guide and console him. Now, four years after his mother's death, he dreamt of her. He was surprised and said he thought she was dead. "I died, but I'm alive," she answered. She told him that she was very happy but had not gone straight to heaven. Why was she so happy, he wanted to know. In answer, she glowed like the sun and began to sing so beautifully that his heart was pierced by sweetness. "I'll be waiting for you. We two must always be together," she said before she left him. Don Bosco awoke, immeasurably consoled.[1]

Margarita Occhiena was born on April 1, 1788, in Capriglio, Italy. Margarita learned the art of homemaking early in life.

155

She was put in charge of her younger brothers and sisters after her father was called up for military service under Napoleon. Left on her own with great responsibility, at an early age, she learned to be competent and to rely on her own capabilities and judgment. This early training was invaluable in later years.

The young Margarita, though attractive and endowed with a spunky personality, was in no hurry to get married. Suitors were avoided. She would walk with one of the ugly, unpleasant, or older women in order to discourage the young men from falling into step beside them. If one did so anyway, she walked so fast he couldn't keep up and had to walk with her companion.

One widower, Francis Bosco—with a young son, an old mother, and a house to keep up—asked her to marry but was refused. Margarita's family and friends began to pressure her; after all, she was twenty-four. It was time that she settled down. Her father, having returned from the army, encouraged her to marry since he could take care of himself. With no fanfare, Margarita and Francis were married on June 6, 1812.

This year was momentous for Napoleon's empire. It was the year of his ignominious retreat across the Russian steppes. Thousands of Italians had already died in the Spanish or Russian wars. His days as emperor were numbered.

A year later Joseph, her first son, was born. Two years after that another son was born on August 16, 1815—the year the great Napoleon was banished to St. Helena. John Melchior Bosco is known to posterity as Don Bosco, the great apostle to youth.

When he was two, his father died of pneumonia, and Margarita had to put to use all the lessons she had learned when caring for her own brothers and sisters. They lived in a small house near their fields. Antonio, her stepson, was ten, and able to help out a great deal. Famine struck the beautiful

Piedmont valley hard. In fields and ditches, men were found dead from starvation with their mouths full of half-chewed grass. Food ran out, and none could be found, so Margarita sacrificed one of her most important assets: her only calf.

Despite the famine, or perhaps because of it, Margarita would not refuse any request for help whether it was for food, medicine, or fuel. She asked for nothing in return. In fact, it seems that it was impossible to give Margarita anything. The little family housed refugees and travelers, even if it meant less food for them. She would even give hospitality to bandits, since she never refused to help anyone. By the same principle, the police would also be welcome to rest and have something to drink. It made for interesting times.

She taught John how to recognize medicinal herbs and how to use them to make healing brews. She brought them to the sick and took care of their needs.

Her main concerns were for her children and the farm. The children she kept scrubbed and tidy. Neatness was a habit with them for the rest of their lives. She refused to let them wear pigtails, which were all the rage, telling them that their curls were handsome enough.

Just as modesty and discretion were important to her as a young woman, so she wanted them to be to her sons. Fearlessly she would rebuke salesmen with indecent books or men telling off-color jokes. "You know I love you more than anything in this world. But I would rather see the Lord take you this instant than have you grow up to become like that wicked man," she told the boys. "I'd strangle you with my own two hands before I'd let that happen!"[2]

LIFE WITH HER YOUNG SONS

Prayer was as essential as eating. As soon as they could talk, the children were taught to pray. Her obvious peace and happiness while praying greatly influenced the two younger boys, but Antonio literally had to be dragged to prayer.

She taught them about God from what they saw around them. Sensitive to beauty, she would point out the loveliness of creation as a sign of God's love for humanity. Catechism lessons came out of conversations: where are heaven and hell? How can we please God? She would tell them Bible stories and tell them the lives of saints. John's captivating storytelling ability was inherited from his mother. "God sees you" was her constant admonition and warning.

Each of the three boys had a different temperament, so Margarita responded differently to each of them. Antonio was sullen, angry, and bossy. He felt that the farm was his, or ought to be, and the others were mere interlopers. He bullied the two younger brothers and told his mother that she did not mean anything more than a stepmother to him.

Once he refused to forgive his brothers for some trivial matter. While they were praying the Our Father, Margarita stopped at the words, "Forgive us our trespasses . . ." and said, "You'd better not say those words, Antonio." He demanded why not. "Say whatever you like but not those words. Coming from you those words would be a lie, even an insult to God. How can you expect God to forgive you when you refuse to forgive others?" He immediately repented.

Joseph was an easier child, except he would occasionally have tantrums. She would hold on to one arm and let him thrash about as much as he liked. "You're wasting your time. Even if you lie there all day I won't let you go. I'm stronger than you. You can't win." He learned that she meant it, and with a smile he'd get up.

John was John. Perhaps because he was her last, he was her favorite. She was just as tough on him when he misbehaved, but she had greater hopes for him. He was rash and acted without thinking.

One day Joseph and John were tending a gobble of turkeys. A stranger tricked them into selling him a turkey for ninety-five cents. He made it sound like a fortune and that their mother would be so pleased. John picked out the fattest one he could find. Margarita was not pleased: the turkey would have brought ten times that much on the market. At her reaction, the boys took off to find the man, leaving the other turkeys unguarded. When they came back the rest of the turkeys were gone as well. They were frantic, but no matter where they looked they could not find them.

Margarita said, "First you let a thief steal one of the turkeys, then you run off to find him, forget all about the other turkeys, and end up by losing not one but a dozen!" She let the gravity of their fault sink in. Then she reassured them.[3]

She taught the boys how to care for animals. John loved nests and she showed him how to build cages for wild birds. She let him keep a screech owl as a pet. When it died from over-feeding, she did not fail to drive home the point. "Gluttons die young because intemperance shortens their lives."

Margarita took the boys to fairs, and John decided to become an acrobat. She let him, but told him he would have to pay for every bit of it himself. He did and set up his own preaching and acrobatic shows.

At age nine he had the guiding vision of his life. He was in a field with boys all around him. Some were happy, others were angry—fighting and cursing. John was angry at the boys for using bad language, so he started fighting them. A regal looking man appeared, and the children stopped fighting. He called John over to him by name and told him to be the boys' leader, but by gentleness and not violence. "Teach them that sin is evil and purity is a precious gift."

John was still angry and upset. "Who are you to tell me to do all these difficult things? They are impossible."

"What seems to you impossible you will make possible, if you choose, by obedience and study," the man replied.

John asked where he could get the knowledge and was told that the man would give him a mistress who would teach him. John asked who the man was. "I am the Son of Heaven whom your mother teaches you to salute three times a day."

A beautiful lady appeared and the man disappeared, while all the boys turned into dogs, wolves, and all kinds of wild creatures. "Don't be afraid, the miracle I work on these animals you shall work on my children. This is your field, the field in which you must labor. Make yourself humble, strong, vigorous." At that all the animals became lambs playing around her feet.

John started to cry, "I don't understand!" and the Lady comforted him.

"Don't worry. You will understand everything in good time."[4]

In the morning John told his family and asked them what they thought it meant. Antonio suggested he would be a bandit chief, obviously thinking it was all a joke. Joseph, simple and prosaic, thought it meant John would be a shepherd. Margarita thought maybe he was called to be a priest. Grandmother said firmly, "You should not pay attention to dreams."

Because his mother had suggested he might be a priest, John felt that he could confide his deepest longing to her. That was exactly what he wanted: to be a priest. "That won't be easy. Do you even know why you want to be a priest?" He did. He said, to evangelize children. Well, then, he would have to get an education, she determined.

In that area, in those days, formal religious instruction was for the rich or townsfolk. Peasants like the Boscos learned from their mother, if she wanted to teach them. Margarita worked carefully with her boys to prepare them for their First Communion. She worked with them, going over the teachings carefully so that any difficulty they had was explained. They were brought to confession frequently.

John went three times in Lent before his First Communion. She taught him how to do an examination of conscience and helped him to apply it to his life. Because John was so advanced, he was allowed to make his two years earlier, at age ten.

In order to prepare for it, his mother suggested he take Easter Sunday as sort of a retreat. He was excused from chores that day. He spoke to no one and spent the day reading and praying. "You are beginning a new life. Guard yourself and become better," Margarita told him. The next Sunday he made his First Communion.

John took the first steps toward an education, but Antonio, like a mountain, was determined to block his way. Margarita fought persistently. Finally, they reached a compromise; in the winter John would study, since there was not any work to do on the farm anyway. The rest of the year he was to work on the farm. Antonio could not stand the sight of John studying at any odd moment. He thought it was foolish impertinence for a peasant to think of becoming a priest. Things came to an impasse, and Margarita told John to leave the house and find work and lodging at another farm. It was the middle of winter when he left.

How can Margarita have sent her beloved son away in seeming preference of Antonio? Because she realized that no peace could be made between the two. John had a habit of making sharp, witty remarks at Antonio's expense— remarks that got Antonio into a rage. Margarita feared that one of these times John would come to physical harm. She couldn't send Antonio away—he legally owned half the farm. Therefore, John had to go. Later, when Antonio came of age he split the property in half. They still lived in the same house, Antonio on the east side and the rest of the family on the west.

For two years, John learned as best he could and worked here and there. Don (an honorary title for a priest much like "father") Calosso came to John's rescue and taught him Latin and other subjects and gave him a place to live. This lasted until Calosso died in 1830. Margarita continued to try to find ways for John to pursue his education. Joseph moved to Sussambrino to work as a sharecropper, and Margarita went with him. John began school at Castelnuovo, which meant great sacrifices for the whole family. Margarita made arrangements for his meals, his board, and his tuition. He was fifteen and basically on his own throughout the semesters.

The next year he moved on to Chieri for four years of high school. At the end of that he had to decide either to join an order or be a diocesan priest. The idea of an order was attractive since they would pay for his education, board, and lodging. He would be more removed from the affairs of the world, and that was very appealing to him. But he would not be able to take care of his mother financially in her old age. She urged him to reason it out carefully but not to worry about her. "I want nothing from you, I expect nothing from you. I was born poor, I live poor, and I wish to die poor. But remember this: if, by some misfortune, you become a rich priest I will never darken your doorstep!"[5]

He received the cassock at age twenty with his mother, benefactors, and a great crowd of boys he had befriended looking on. Margarita said to him, as he left for the secular seminary in 1835, "My son, you are now dressed as a priest. The greatest satisfaction a mother can ever feel is mine at this moment. But it is not the cassock but holiness that makes you respected. Remember, if you ever begin to doubt your vocation that you do nothing to dishonor your Maker. I would rather you stay a peasant than to see you a priest who had forgotten his duty."[6]

Both of them were near tears. She went on to say, "When you were born I consecrated you to Our Lady. When you began your studies, I told you to be devoted to her. Now I ask you to be entirely hers. Choose your friends among those who love her, and if you do become a priest, spread devotion to her."[7]

THE MINISTRY OF MOTHERHOOD

In June of 1841 John Bosco was ordained a priest. His mother told him, "Remember, John, to begin to say Mass is to begin to suffer. . . . I am sure that you will pray for me every day and I want nothing more. Never worry about me. From now on you must think only of saving souls."[8]

Don Bosco quickly fell into the pattern of his ministry with boys. He gathered a group of young street boys on Sunday morning for confession and Mass. In the afternoon, they would regroup for games, catechism, and stories. This pattern of religion and recreation formed the oratory, as he called it. He visited the boys at work and spent time talking to them in the streets.

The work was successful, and the number of boys grew and grew. He had to find bigger and bigger places for them to meet in. Of course, those who lived closest to his meeting places did not appreciate their Sabbath rest being broken by the sound of over a hundred rowdy boys having fun under their windows. Finally, he was able to situate them in a field and two-story house. The year was 1846. The house was double-sided, and on the other side was a brothel. Hardly ideal surroundings for a priest and boys.

Following this he contracted pneumonia and almost died. At the end of two weeks, he went home to his mother to convalesce. He knew that she would take care of him.

After three months he was well enough to return, but he needed a housekeeper—one that would not mind living in a slum next to a house of prostitution. A priest friend suggested Margarita, but Don Bosco did not see how he could. After all, she was fifty-eight years old. She was finally done with all her work of mothering and able to hand over the heavy load to Joseph's wife. She was surrounded by her grandchildren and friends. She would have to leave the house and field that she fought so hard to keep in those first years. Would it be fair? Would it be just?

Then again, was it the will of God? So he asked her. Margarita said that if it would please the Lord, she was ready to go. She, along with Don Bosco, left after the Feast of All Saints.

Margarita sent wheat, corn, beans, chestnuts, and vegetables ahead of them. She carried baskets of linens and kitchen utensils. Don Bosco carried his breviary and a missal. They walked all the way to Voldocca and arrived in the evening.

Her new home was four tiny rooms, two of which were bare. Their total possessions amounted to two beds, two benches, one crucifix, a blessed palm, a statue of Mary, a small table, a trunk, cooking pot, two saucepans, and some plates. She thought since there was so little it wouldn't take much to care for it. She could not have been more wrong.

Don Bosco was without a regular source of income and lived on donations for his work. They were not sufficient to keep both of them alive, yet requests for help kept coming in. They began to sell off their small inheritances. Don Bosco could not afford vestments, so Margarita made them for her son out of her wedding dress. She paid the rent with the only jewelry she had ever owned: her wedding ring and small gold necklace. "When I looked at those things which I was holding in my hands for the last time, at first I felt a little upset. . . . But, afterward, I felt so happy that if I had a hundred trousseaux I'd have given them all up for the same purpose without the least regard."[9]

Within a short while, he began taking in homeless boys to sleep at night. One night he brought home twelve boys and asked Margarita to fix them something to eat. Then he sent them off to the loft. The next morning he went early to wake them up and found that they had absconded with the sheets, pillowcases, and blankets. Margarita scolded him for being so trusting and attempting such a rash scheme. Of course, Margarita did the same thing the next week herself. Rashness ran in the family.

A few days later she came across a young bricklayer's assistant who was soaking wet. She dried him off, gave him some food and a change of clothing and bedded him down in the kitchen. She spoke to him a few simple words about God's love and how to be good for him in return. Then the three of them—Don Bosco, his mother, and the first of hundreds of boys who would live with them—said their prayers and went to sleep.

LIFE IN THE PINARDI HOUSE

Don Bosco ended up buying the entire Pinardi house, and thirty boys lived with them in their home. Margarita cooked a thick soup for all of them every day. There were now between six and seven hundred boys in the Oratory; they played in the field next to the house. Between the playing field and the house was Mamma Margarita's vegetable garden. It was the one thing she was terribly proud of and protective about. One Sunday the boys, in the middle of a great pretend battle, overran and totally destroyed it. It was the last straw, and she wept. On another occasion, they tore down the clothes she had hung up to dry and trampled them. They lost some of the clothes and ripped others. They took her things and didn't return them. And the noise! The constant comings and goings! Some of them would be rude or disobedient to her. Margarita would get up early in the morning to care for the boys before they left for work. She did chores, prepared the noon meal for perhaps a hundred or so, did more dishes, cleaned, shopped, then prepared the evening meal. Night time gave her an opportunity to do the mending by an oil lamp. She was exhausted. She begged her son to be allowed to go home and live in peace. His success was killing her.

"Certainly, Mother. You are absolutely right," Don Bosco said and pointed to the crucifix on the wall. "But . . ." She stared at the slain Christ and then at her son, picked up her apron, and went back to work.

The work went on, heavy, intense, and rewarding. The boys came to them with vermin, open sores, ragged clothes, starving for food and for love. They were transformed under the care of this mother and her son. She was mother, a benevolent tyrant, more their mother than their physical mothers.

She ran their lives and ruled their hearts. Her power was based on her love for them. She would scold them and give it to them straight—no sweet pious phrases for her. "Don Bosco sweats blood to offer you a chance in life and you throw it away!" she said to one lazy scholar. "Only the animals act the way you do," she said to a frequent fighter. "Can't you see that your companions are your brothers?"

If rich and important people came to visit Don Bosco, she would greet them but continue with her sewing. If she thought they stayed too long, she started to pray in an undertone. They usually got the message. She would refuse a pinch of snuff because she didn't want to catch an expensive habit. But offer her a snuffbox, at least a costly one, and she'd take that to sell for food.

She could have had it a little easier. She could have insisted on more help. Time and time again, Don Bosco would give her money to buy a new dress, but she would spend it on the boys. When she died, the money her son had given her for a new bonnet was found in her pocket.

In 1850 the work was finally too much for her, and her sister Marianne moved in to help. Six years later, in the middle of November, Mamma Margarita came down with pneumonia. She would not recover.

She called Don Bosco to her bedside and asked to speak to him alone. "What I'm going to say, I say with the same sincerity I'd use in the confessional. I hope it will help you understand the Oratory better." The peasant mother was telling her son, the founder, how to understand his own order better! She discussed in frank and open detail his coworkers; those he could trust and those he couldn't, and those who could betray him. She emphasized that poverty must be the hallmark of his life and of the work he did.

Then she said to him: "There was a time I helped you receive the sacraments. Now it's your turn to help me. Let's recite the prayers for the dying together."

Her elder son Joseph was there as well. She was in her agony and asked Don Bosco to leave the room because his grief was making her suffer twice as much. He returned shortly, "A son should not leave his mother at a moment like this," he told her.

"You won't be able to stand it," she retorted. "I'm asking you this one favor. It's the last I'll ever ask of you. Leave me. When you suffer, you only double my pain. Leave me and pray for me. That's all I ask. Good-bye, John."[10]

They were the last words she spoke to him. By three o'clock in the morning, on the twenty-fifth of November, Mamma Margarita was dead. Don Bosco hurried to church and said a Mass for the repose of her soul.

Her whole life had been one lovely litany of loving. God had prepared her for this life, as much as she might complain in the midst of trying circumstances. Margarita had been forced by circumstances to shoulder responsibilities beyond her years. She married into a challenging situation. She gave and gave to all who asked for her help. And she believed in her son and her God. With a heart so given to him, how could Jesus do less than to give her more of his love, his service, and his cross?

Mamma Margarita's life is not one that most of us would choose. It is easy to look at motherhood with a job mentality: "When the kids are grown I'll finally be free to take up my own life again." Mamma Margarita proves that motherhood is not a job, it's a vocation—a holy calling that continues until our children die. God may even give us children besides our own to love.

✦ FOR YOUR LIFE ✦

- Neatness was a habit Margarita taught her children early in life.

- She fearlessly rebuked men for telling off-color jokes or stories or showing pornographic literature. She both set an example for her sons and protected their innocence.

- She used ordinary questions the boys asked to teach them about God.

- She disciplined each of her sons according to his temperament.

ELEVEN

"She Prepared
Her Daughters to Die"
St. Elizabeth Ann Seton

Few saints have found their lives so interwoven with death as Mother Seton's was. Her great faith in God was fashioned and perfected as she prepared her loved ones to die.

ELIZABETH ANN BAYLEY SETON was born on August 28, 1774, in New York City. Her mother died three years later. The American Revolution boomed away in the background of her early childhood but had surprisingly little direct impact on her daily life. Her doctor father, totally absorbed in medical research, married again. For reasons unknown, he completely shut out his daughters from his first marriage, though he scarcely paid more attention to the seven children his second wife bore him. Marital tensions grew, and eventually Dr. Bayley and his wife were separated. Elizabeth and her older sister Mary spent a great deal of time, anywhere from four to eight years, living at their Uncle William and Aunt Sarah Bayley's house in New Rochelle.

Excluded from the love of a closeknit family, Betty, as

Elizabeth was called, grew up lonely. As a result, she loved solitude and thought long and deeply about life. Raised as an Episcopalian, Betty found as much comfort and knowledge of God from nature as she did from her church. She fell in love with the Bible when she read it as a teenager and found it to be her lasting source of joy, hope, and consolation.

All was not completely grim: there were picnics, skating, sledding parties, and dances in her life. She began to take an interest in boys and looked forward to getting married one day.

In spite of losing her mother and suffering her father's indifference, Elizabeth never hardened her heart or became pessimistic. She had the grace to accept her father with his failings and continue to love him just the same. In 1790 she returned to live with other relatives in New York, and her father began to return Elizabeth's affection. Their relationship, finally, became healthy and loving.

During these years, Elizabeth fell in love with William Magee Seton—six years her senior and the son of a wealthy merchant. They were married January 25, 1794, and her life became filled with everything she had lacked until then.

Now Elizabeth would know love in overflowing, heaped-up measure, for the Setons dearly loved her. Her husband doted on her and she on him.

Another great joy was the pleasure of moving into a house at 27 Wall Street a year after her wedding. "My own home at twenty—that and heaven too, quite impossible!" she wrote years later. "So every moment [was] clouded with that fear, 'My God, if I enjoy this I lose you'—yet no true thought of who [sic] I would lose, rather fear of hell and [being] shut out of heaven."[1] How could it be right to be this happy?

The healthy births of a daughter, Anna, in 1795, and a son, William, nineteen months later, made her happiness complete. Elizabeth reveled in home, family, and housekeeping.

She was full of laughter, a quality she never lost even in

the most difficult times in her life. Charming, intelligent, pretty, and lively, Elizabeth was also endowed with a fierce temper—a quality her daughter Anna inherited. She was happiest spending the evening reading books and writing letters to her family and friends.

When William was about nine months old, he was so sick that his grandfather, Dr. Bayley, was certain he would die. As with all mothers, Elizabeth struggled with fear and anxiety until he began to get better. In her darkest moment, she almost wished that God had not given her the gift of motherhood because of the enormity of her suffering as she watched him suffer.

Seventeen ninety-eight ushered in a series of misfortunes that would try Elizabeth's faith in God enormously. The senior William Seton died, and Will and Elizabeth took responsibility for the seven brothers and sisters still at home. Business troubles beset them, culminating in bankruptcy two years later. Elizabeth had a difficult third pregnancy and delivery during which both the mother and child almost died. In order to help support the family, she had to take on a great deal of the business letters and family papers as her husband tried to settle his father's estate and save the family business. Over the next year, sickness would strike first one family member and then another as they suffered from smallpox and yellow fever. Business troubles mounted, and Will's health grew worse. He became increasingly despondent and anxious. Elizabeth proved to be his main moral support during those days of trial.

She struggled to become the mother of seven, plus her own three, when she was only twenty-four years old. At times, her letters reveal a discouragement with life that mothers of even two or three are familiar with. Giving up her own home and quiet life was extremely hard on her. One radiant blessing emerged: Elizabeth and her sister-in-law Rebecca, age eighteen, became fast friends for life. Elizabeth called her "Soul's Sister."

Elizabeth was the kind of person, however, who is able to bear greater things more easily than lesser troubles. At times, even this natural courage wavered as Will constantly worried about what would become of them, particularly since "them" was such a large number.

A fourth child, Catherine, was born in 1799, and Will began bankruptcy proceedings that fall. In May they had to move out of the big house on Stone Street, in a well-to-do neighborhood, and into the Battery—a lowerclass one. During these years, Elizabeth taught the children at home since schools were too costly. That summer her father died after a sudden illness.

A veritable whirlwind of adversity had tried her, but it did not defeat her: death, financial ruin, loss of status, a difficult pregnancy, and her childrens' and husband's sickness. Like a hot, sultry spell in July quickly ripens fruit, adversity forced her to mature in character and spirituality. "... I think the greatest happiness of this life is to be released from the cares and formalities of what is called the world. My world is my family, and all the change to me will be that I can devote myself unmolested to my treasure . . . for the present season, while the cloud hangs heaviest, I trust where my trust has never yet failed."[2]

Elizabeth did not bear these things alone, supported only by invisible, immaterial grace. Rather God used elements in the world around her to refresh, sustain, and strengthen her. These same things continued to support her during all the difficulties of her life.

Nature was a never-ceasing consolation to her, the young mother, as it had been to her as a lonely child. The summers spent in the country or on Staten Island were periods of refreshment for her soul. She loved to take walks by herself before anyone was up or after the children were in bed. Beauty, as much as friendship, was necessary for her well-being.

Reading during these times of stress was another source

of strength and consolation. She often read her Bible for two hours a day. Sometimes she would mark passages in her books that she looked forward to sharing with her children when they were older.

Friendship was critical for her especially during these times of stress. Nursing a sick friend not only gave her a chance to show her love but, as she realized, helped take her mind off her own struggles. But she was able to share her own fears and worries as well as bear those of others, and this brought others close to her. Far from being absorbed by her own trials, Elizabeth chose to become involved in the Widows' Society, a charity she had helped found. Her own troubles were put in perspective by exposure to others' problems, and gratitude to God was the result. She made a habit of spending New Year's Eve in "contemplating and tracing the boundless mercy of God" through the past year.

Motherhood itself was a source of joy and consolation to her. She delighted in the children and was enchanted at each stage of their childhood. Her love of motherhood would become key to her understanding of God as Father and of the church.

In 1802 Rebecca, her last child, was born and Elizabeth experienced a deepening of faith. Yet Will's health began to decline rapidly in 1803 and plans were made for the time-honored remedy for tuberculosis, a sea voyage. All the children, except Anna Marie, were farmed out to various relatives for the duration of the trip. The slightest chance of her husband's recovery was worth the separation from her children, but that did not mean it did not hurt her terribly. Elizabeth's last words to her friend Eliza Sadler were, "Take my darlings often in your arms!"

The Setons arrived in Leghorn, Italy, expecting to disembark and go to their friends, the Filicchis, to stay. Instead they were put into quarantine, or the *lazaretto*, a dank, cold, and drafty place. Will was terribly ill, and it seemed as though he could die at any moment. Elizabeth was overcome with tears. All three of them cried until Elizabeth's eyes smarted. She found a little room to pray in and emptied her heart out to God; then she went back to care for her husband and child. For one month, she would have to take care of Will and entertain Anna by herself in a bare room. An Italian servant, Louis, would help with cooking. During this time Will almost died twice but rallied each time.

One day she was in an "agony of sorrow" and could not even be comforted at prayer until she realized that she was "offending my only friend and resource in my misery, and voluntarily shutting out from my soul the only consolation it could receive." The next day she realized that their difficult predicament had to be God's will for them and began to search the Scriptures in between jumping rope to keep herself warm. She wrote, "Looked around our prison and found that its situation was beautiful." Two days later she wrote, "Not only willing to take my cross, but kissed it, too." The next, "I find my present opportunity a treasure, and my confinement of body a liberty of soul, which I may never again enjoy while they are united." Will, too, called this "the only time which he has not lost." These days in prison brought the three of them closer than they ever had been to each other and to God.

HER CONVERSION TO CATHOLICISM

Finally, a month after they landed the Setons were released and went to Pisa to a lodging house. The next day Will entered his final agony and died on the morning of December 27. Changes in sailing dates and a bout of scarlet fever for Anna Marie kept the two of them in Italy for several months. Elizabeth grew increasingly homesick for her children, but God's purpose for bringing her to Italy and keeping her there became clear. It was during this time that she became intellectually convinced of the truth of Catholicism.

Motherhood, ordinary family life, her children's words and experiences became the most common way God would use to teach her about himself. She saw in her children a pattern of how she should be a child of her heavenly Father.

Beloved Kate, I will take you, then, for my pattern, and try to please Him as you to please me. To grieve with a like tenderness when I displease Him, to obey and mind His voice as you do mine. To do my work as neatly and exactly as you do yours, grieve to lose sight of Him for a moment, fly with joy to meet Him, fear He should go and leave me even when I sleep—this is the lesson of love you set me. And when I have seemed to be angry, without petulance or obstinacy you silently and steadily try to accomplish my wish. I will say "Dearest Lord, give me grace to copy well this lovely image of my duty to Thee."
. . . The bands of nature and grace all twined together. The parent offers the child, the child the parent, and both are united in the source of their being and rest together on redeeming love.[3]

Motherhood was the concept that helped Elizabeth understand the Blessed Virgin Mary, traditionally very difficult for Protestants to accept. The motherhood of Mary also healed a painful lack in Elizabeth's life: ". . . I felt really I had a Mother—which you know my foolish heart so often lamented to have lost in early days.

"From the first remembrance of infancy, I have looked, in all the plays of childhood and wildness of youth, to the clouds for my mother; and at that moment, it seemed as if I had found more than her, even in tenderness and pity of a mother. So I cried myself to sleep on her heart."[4]

Elizabeth and Anna Marie finally sailed for New York in April of 1804. All her children were waiting for their mother and sister as the boat docked in New York. As happy as she was to find them all alive and well, she was distraught to find her beloved sister-in-law Rebecca dying from tuberculosis.

To come from the deathbed of her husband to that of her soul sister was a great blow.

Her convictions shaken by the arguments of friends and her pastor, Elizabeth wavered for a year before she finally converted to Catholicism. She firmly believed that her children would only be saved by embracing the Catholic faith. [Note to the reader: We need to remember that this was long before the spirit of ecumenism ushered in by the Second Vatican Council. The Catholic church now recognizes that other Christians who are validly baptized and remain faithful to Christ are on their way to salvation, although they lack the fullness of truth found in the Catholic church.] But her children's financial well-being seemed diametrically opposed to that consideration. Her wealthy godmother, Mrs. Startin, and a rich uncle had both named her sole heir in their wills. Conversion meant being cut out of the wills, yet her children's eternal salvation meant more to her than their temporal loss. Elizabeth was willing to pay the price of monetary loss for that great gain.

Already the lack of a father was influencing her sons: William, ten; and Richard, eight. "My saucy boys almost master me," she wrote to her friend Julia Scott. She attempted to solve the problem by sending them to a Jesuit-run boys' school in Georgetown.

Anna Marie made her First Communion during a veritable hurricane of a family quarrel over the conversion of Cecilia Seton—one of Will's younger sisters. To Elizabeth, Anna's First Communion was her coming-of-age. No longer would she merely be a mother to her, but a friend and companion in the faith as well. She wrote a note to Anna during the last week of preparation: ". . . you have it in your power to make me the happiest of mothers and to be my sweet comfort through every sorrow, or to occasion the heaviest affliction to my poor soul that it can meet within this world.

"And as your example will have the greatest influence on

your dear little sisters also, and you do not know how soon you may be in the place of their mother to them, your doing your duty faithfully is of the greatest consequence, besides what you owe to God and to your own soul. . . .''[5]

Writing notes to her children was a habit with Elizabeth. She would encourage, inspire, or correct them as needed to reinforce what she had told them. It was another way that she could show her love for each child. They, in turn, wrote notes back to her.

Elizabeth was also concerned at the effect that the young boarders were having on her girls. She thought more of moving either to Canada or Baltimore. Fr. Dubourg, the president of St. Mary's College in Baltimore, proposed that she come to Baltimore and teach. She began a small school next to the Sulpician Chapel just outside the city in the summer of 1808. Finances were much easier, and there was a great deal of peace and joy in her surroundings. The children were doing very well. Those in charge of her boys were happy with their conduct and studies. Anna was developing into a highly accomplished young woman and was just as lovely as her mother. Kit was not healthy, but neither was she very ill. Brighter than her siblings, she was also a very affectionate child. Rebecca was plainer than the other two but had a sweeter disposition. Elizabeth's greatest delight was to have all her children around her again. Baltimore was a much more Catholic town. The people warmly and lovingly welcomed the Setons into their midst. Unfortunately, Elizabeth's health declined and became a constant source of worry for her children.

FOUNDING THE FIRST AMERICAN SISTERHOOD

From the beginning, teaching school was only part of God's plan for Elizabeth Seton. The idea of an American sisterhood had been born along with the idea of the day school. "It is expected that I shall be the mother of many daughters," she wrote to Cecilia back in New York. Cecilia and her older sister Harriet came to join Elizabeth.

Yet never did she consider abandoning her children. Yes, she would be a religious sister, but one with children. Just as St. Jeanne de Chantal questioned herself at times, Elizabeth wondered if she could do both. At every point, she once again realized that God would bring about his perfect will. If he wanted her to be the head of this congregation, then she would; if not, he would tell her so. She let the Spirit of God convince those in authority over her. Later, when discussion arose over her leadership of the congregation, she made her position perfectly clear: "... you know I would gladly make every sacrifice you think consistent with my first and inseparable obligations as a mother." The decision to found the Daughters of Charity began to move forward quickly. Meanwhile, Anna Marie had fallen in love at thirteen.

Elizabeth had been concerned for two years about her daughter's increasing beauty and physical maturity. From that point on she had chaperoned her all the more closely. Her surprise was as great as her sense of betrayal when Anna finally told her mother about her beau. She and the young man, Charles Du Pavillon, had fallen in love in chapel by glances and smiles. They convinced Will and Dick to pass notes back and forth between the two of them. He was much older than she was—a good young man who should have known better. Elizabeth was upset because Anna was too young and because it had gone on behind her back—which was probably half the fun of the affair for the pair. At that time, it was very improper for young girls to accept love notes and bouquets from admirers without permission from their parents.

Shocked and hurt at first, Elizabeth confided her heartache to Julia Scott but continued to act lovingly toward Anna: "... what could a doting and unhappy mother do but take the part of friend and confidant, dissembling my distress and resolving that—if there was no remedy—to help her at least by my love and pity." Julia told Elizabeth that she was overly concerned. She should worry more about the worldly girls Anna associated with than her present infatuation.

Elizabeth allowed the sweethearts to meet once under her supervision and set up rules of conduct. There were to be no more love letters between the two, while the Setons still lived in Baltimore. Once they moved to Emmitsburg, Charles could write but had to send the letters unsealed in an envelope addressed to Elizabeth.

Like many mothers, Elizabeth felt anger, betrayal, and hurt, but she would not make her daughter feel guilty. Instead, she tried all the harder to show her love and understanding, even while making firm rules of conduct for the relationship.

The impending move to Emmitsburg was timely, as she wrote to Julia Scott: "This pleases me for many reasons. In the first place, I shall live in the mountains; in the next, I shall see no more of the world than if I was out of it, and have every object centered in my own family, both of provision, employment, etc. . . . For if *young D.* is hereafter true to his attachment, he may easily claim her; if not, her happiness depends on seeing him no more."[6]

On March 25, 1809, the Feast of the Annunciation, Elizabeth Ann Seton took vows of poverty, chastity, and obedience before Archbishop Carroll and was known as Mother Seton from then on.

The move to Emmitsburg took place in late June. The sisters, six in number—Cecilia and Harriet Seton, her younger stepsisters, and the three young Seton children—lived in Stone House outside of town. Nine more women joined them in the next few months, which made the accommodations very cramped. A new house was begun immediately to contain both school and convent. But troubles quickly flared up for this new family of Elizabeth's.

Illness, the removal of the order's beloved confessor, and problems with the priest superiors of the order taxed Elizabeth's patience and faith. She learned to fight for her spiritual children's well-being as she had for her own sons and daughters in New York.

Anna was still her mother's problem child. She wrote to Julia Scott: "If you had her she would be a source of perpetual uneasiness to you, for as she grows up and looses herself from that blind obedience exacted from a child under thirteen, she takes many varieties of temper, which makes her disposition so unequal that, until she is more matured and experience teaches her some necessary lessons, it is very difficult to make her happy. The great error, now past and irreparable, on my part is to have made her my friend and companion too soon."[7]

The days of the *lazaretto*, the early death of her father, and the many hardships of life had taken their toll. Elizabeth had always had difficulty with the headstrong and quick-tempered girl. Making a confidant out of her, sharing with Anna her joys and sorrows, insights and thoughts, seemed the best course of action to draw her daughter to her and help Anna control those qualities. Now Elizabeth saw that she had gone overboard and the resulting overfamiliarity had bred a certain amount of contempt.

Yet despite Anna's teenage storms of emotion, the family was together and happy. Family gatherings were held weekly with the boys coming over from their school. Everyone would gather in the small dining room for a hearty meal and much laughter and fun. Richard was the clown, and Bec was lively and funloving. Kitty and William were more serious and sedate. They all got along very well together, though they had their spats.

Late that fall William grew so ill that a shroud was made. But after he had received the last sacraments, he began to get better. Cecilia, always in precarious health, got steadily worse. But the great shock was Harriet's sudden death.

Succumbing to some sort of "brain fever," she died three days before Christmas.

Great joy and sorrow followed: that winter the first parochial school in America was founded by the fledging congregation. Then, shortly after Easter, Cecilia died. The last of the three beloved sisters-in-law whom Elizabeth had raised as daughters and loved as sisters had died. She broke the news bravely in her letters, but her sister Mary Post read between the lines and wrote back, "Knowing that you possess an unusual degree of fortitude does not hide from me the conflicts of mind you endure when your feelings are excited by those who are dear to you."

A saint is not someone who is free from the emotions that shake our human frame but one who goes through them to the heart of God.

Anna had decided to stay in Baltimore to try her wings, and Elizabeth allowed her to do so, though she had misgivings. The young girl soon realized that she was "almost" as unhappy in the city as she had been at the mountain. She missed her mother and wanted to come home after all. Anna realized that even though her mother had been kind and understanding, she never had really approved of the relationship. As it turned out, there was good cause. Within months Charles Du Pavillon wrote to tell her he had fallen in love with another girl and was marrying her. Anna, because Elizabeth had kept communication open and loving, was able to turn to her in her sorrow, and they became even closer.

Instead of finding the school and the sisters' life unbearably boring as she did before, Anna took an interest in the youngest pupils. Mother and daughter took long horseback rides together, enjoying nature and each other's company. Anna was very quiet in her grief that autumn and then decided to join the sisterhood. The dramatic touch was as evident here as in her romantic and clandestine love affair, but at the heart of it there was a genuine vocation.

Troubles with the Superior, Fr. David, continued and threatened to split the community apart. The winter had been extremely hard on the women's health. Elizabeth had finally admitted that she had consumption. Tuberculosis was spreading through the sisters. With organizational troubles, factions between sisters, and ill health, Elizabeth was hard pressed—but not enough to forget her children.

PREPARING HER CHILDREN FOR DEATH

Just as Anna's heart was settled, her health gave way. The next few years would tax Elizabeth's emotional strength and trust in God considerably, as two of her girls suffered and died from tuberculosis, while her boys gave her increasing cause for concern. William was so sick that he could not be moved from Mount St. Mary's College. Anna was just as ill, and Elizabeth did not dare to leave her or the other sick sisters for long.

All the bouts of tuberculosis in the family had left their mark on Elizabeth. She admitted, "[Anna] may not be as ill as I imagine, for never was anyone easier frightened, after so many hard trials." She came down with a painful case of boils and was nearly frantic with worry for her children. Mary Post, a mother herself, wrote to her sister: "children so wind themselves round one's heart so as to almost make one wonder how existence could be supportable without them." As always, it was to God that Elizabeth turned for her comfort and support. Fear gave way time and time again to trust and resignation to God's will.

Elizabeth began to prepare her daughter to die. Eternity was her steadfast hope and only lasting consolation, and it was a spiritual principle that she had passed on to her daughter. They talked as much of happy news, William's return to health, letters from home, as they did of her approaching death. Anna's growth in holiness after her return home nine months previously had been heroic. Her sufferings were horrible to witness: her lungs were consumed and her bones protruded in places. Every breath was an agony. Her mother sat by her side as often as she could. The two of them surpassed the merely human in their love for one another through this final crisis. Elizabeth would call on Anna to offer up her increasing suffering, while Anna would gently scold her mother for crying: "Can it be for me, should you not rejoice? It will be but a moment and [we shall be] reunited for Eternity."

As Anna entered her final agony Elizabeth wrote, ". . . the pain of her eyes was so great she could no longer fix them. She said, 'I can no longer look at you, my dear Crucifix, but I enter my agony with my Saviour . . . yes, adorable Lord, your will and yours alone be done. I will it too. I leave my dearest Mother because you will it.'"[8]

Elizabeth knelt beside the bed holding high the crucifix for her little girl, the "Child of her soul" to see. Finally, she was led by the hand to the chapel to pray before the Blessed Sacrament until her sixteen-year-old daughter died.

Elizabeth was dead to the world in her grief. Yet when the boys arrived sobbing hard, she rebuked them, "You are *men*, and Mother looks for support from you." Thankfully, that attitude about manly emotion has been discarded today. Anna was buried in the "little sacred wood," the third sister to be buried there, and the third Seton. When all was done at graveside, one tear only was seen on Elizabeth's cheek and the impassioned words uttered in a whisper, "Father, Thy will be done!"

Of all the deaths she had endured or would endure, this death was the one that plunged Elizabeth into her greatest grief and desolation. "For three months after Nina (Annina was her pet name) was taken, I was so often expecting to lose my senses, and my head was so disordered, that unless for the daily duties always before me, I did not know much what I did or what I left undone." It was an anguish of the heart—one that hurt to some degree until Elizabeth died, but it was not a despair of soul. She resigned herself to God's will from the first, yet that took nothing away from her motherly grief at losing a child.

The war of 1812 affected the friends of Mother Seton more than it did the sisterhood. The British attacked Baltimore, and Francis Scott Key on a British man-of-war offshore Fort McHenry wrote the poem that became the *Star Spangled Banner*. A second foundation was begun in 1814 when three sisters from Emmitsburg took over an orphanage in Philadelphia.

Meanwhile, Rebecca, Elizabeth's youngest daughter, was already dying so slowly that it was not noticed for quite some time. She had fallen on the ice, before Anna had died, and had seriously injured her hip. But she had minimized the pain to her mother. The last thing she wanted was to add to her mother's worries, so she walked as normally as possible, which only made the problem worse. Medical diagnosis determined that at best she would be permanently crippled. As it turned out, the family consumption settled in her hip.

On top of this, Elizabeth had to cope with young William's decision about a future career. William, age eighteen, wanted to join the Navy, but his mother wanted him to pursue a career in business. She was concerned for his faith if he joined the armed services. She wrote to him: "Be not my dear one so unhappy as to break willfully any command of our God, or to omit your prayers on any account. . . . You cannot ever guess the incessant cry of my soul to them [Jesus and Mary] for you. Don't say Mother has the rest to comfort her. No, no, my dear William, from the first moment I received you in my arms and to my breast you have been consecrated to God by me; and I have never ceased to beg him to take you from this world rather than you should offend him or dishonor your dear soul; and as you know my stroke of death would be to know that you have quitted that path of virtue which alone can reunite us for ever. Separation, everything else I can bear—but that never. Your mother's heart must break if that blow falls on it."[9]

It was a concern that would become a constant refrain in her letters from then on. "My greatest anxiety in life is my poor boys." She knew that her boys were not brilliant. They would not voice an opinion that they thought was different than hers. She knew as well that she tended to be indulgent, pitying them too much for their lack of a father and their difficult childhood. She did everything within her power to be the best mother she could, but she could not be a father. It was this unavoidable lack that caused her to pray all the more fervently to their heavenly Father for his grace, protection, and mercy. Though her sons did not inherit or develop her adamant character and strength of religious devotion and even lived rather mediocre lives, they ended well.

"For many years," she wrote to her friend Antonio Filicchi, "I have had no prayer for my children but that Our Blessed God would do everything to them in the way of affliction and adversity, if only—He will have their souls!" God seems to have answered Elizabeth's prayers for her children. Although in the case of her boys who outlived her, God's answer came years after her own death. Richard died at sea from a fever he contracted while nursing another. William returned to a devout practice of his faith toward the end of his life. His daughter became a nun and his son became a bishop, initiating proceedings for his grandmother's beatification.

Bec was swiftly following her sister Anna as the disease progressed. Elizabeth had learned a new depth of trust in God and no longer had to fight wild bouts of interior rebellion at his ways. Once again she prepared a daughter to die. Once again, the approach of death brought a deeper intimacy and love between mother and daughter. Once again, spiritual maturity ripened quickly before the frost killed it on the vine.

Bec, twelve years old, was sent to Philadelphia for an attempted cure. Elizabeth did her best to reassure her by sharing with her the smallest details of life. She helped her get ready for that more final separation by reminding her of the still more permanent reunion. "My Rebecca, *we* will at last unite in His eternal praise, lost in Him, you and I, closer still than in the nine months so dear when, as I told you, I carried you in my bosom as he is our Virgin Mother's—then, no more separation."

After Bec had returned and her condition worsened, Elizabeth asked Julia to send Rebecca a doll to amuse her. "I am," admitted Elizabeth, "extremely fond of dolls myself." As time went on, she could not stand or lay down but only sit. For nine weeks, Bec took to sitting on her mother's knee and leaning against her all day and most of the night. "We wet each other pretty often with tears." Elizabeth lost all feeling in her left arm, and her legs were so stiff from inactivity that she limped when she did walk.

Richard had by this time set off on his own, while Kitty had gone to Baltimore on an extended visit. Elizabeth wanted Catherine to experience more of the world than the valley she lived in. Consequently, Elizabeth had the bulk of Bec's care. She worried over Bec's readiness for death, she was not blind to her daughter's faults: "little, old, and even saucy ways of pride, pretension, etc. (Seton maladies)." "I tell her, Can you say with a true heart, 'Thy will be done!' 'Oh, that I can,' she answers, brightening with joy, 'if *that* is enough.'" But even in the most excruciating pain, they could laugh together over a silly joke Bec told.

Bec's mind wandered a great deal toward the end. The afternoon before she died, she told her mother, "I have just been handing Our Lord my little cup. It is now quite full. He will come for me." Before dawn on November 3, 1816, Bec asked to sit up once more. "It will be the last struggle."

Her mother and Sister Cecil lifted her up once more. "The darling head fell on its well-known heart it loved so well . . . she said distinctly:

'Ma, the girls talk so loud.'

'Think only of your dear Saviour now, my darling,' I said.

'To be sure, certainly,' she answered, and said no more, dropping her head for the last time on her Mother's heart."

Bec's coffin was laid side-by-side with that of her sister Anna. Elizabeth could see the little graveyard from the windows of the house and took great consolation on looking out upon their graves during the day.

After this death, Elizabeth drew near to the end of her mothering. William had ended up in the Navy after all. Richard was in business. Kit was visiting family and friends for extended periods of time. The sisterhood was flourishing, and there was a waiting list for boarders and day students. While the order was expanding, Elizabeth's health grew worse. She felt as though she lived to pray for all her children.

In the fall of 1820, Elizabeth was confined to bed and expected to die. She loved to listen to the sound of the children playing outside and would have the youngest of them brought in to share a piece of fruit and talk with her.

By God's grace, she had joy in her spiritual children because her own boys neglected her dreadfully during her last days. It was as if God were purifying her attachment to them and helping her to turn them over completely to his Fatherly care.

The end came on January 4, 1821. She slipped silently away as one of the sisters whispered the *Gloria* and *Magnificat* in her ear. Sister Xavier wrote, "It seemed to me that Our Lord was there, near to her, very close, awaiting this good soul." Surely her daughters—natural, adopted, and spiritual—were there to greet her as well.

☙ FOR YOUR LIFE ❧

- Elizabeth put her children's spiritual good ahead of monetary considerations.

- The Bible and daily Eucharist were her constant sources of strength.

- Elizabeth took time for herself to be mentally, emotionally, and spiritually restored by nature.

- She kept up her friendships and gave and drew consolation from them.

- Elizabeth did not let her ministry override her family responsibilities but handled both of them successfully.

- She did not turn against her daughter, Anna, even when she felt hurt, but kept the lines of communication open.

"I Want You to Be a Warrior and Raise Children"
Amy Carmichael

Young, fervent, and unmarried, Amy Carmichael intended to devote her whole life to preaching the gospel. She did it in a most unexpected way: she became the mother of nearly nine hundred children.

O N A SNOWY WINTER'S EVENING in 1892, a young and beautiful Irish girl of twenty-four sat alone in her room. Years of burning concern for the salvation of souls were answered in an irrevocable, insistent call. As plainly as if he had spoken with a human voice, Amy heard God say to her, "GO YE." She went to Southern India where she lived for fifty-seven years.

Amy Beatrice Carmichael was born on December 16, 1867, in Millisle, Ireland. Her parents were staunch Presbyterians who raised Amy and her six brothers and sisters to love God. Her father died from double pneumonia while Amy was still young.

When visiting friends in Scotland in 1886, Amy experienced a deeper relationship with Jesus. Returning to Belfast, she devoted herself to working with the "shawlies," young working girls who wore shawls over their heads because they could not afford hats.

Eventually, she moved to Broughton Grange in England and became the unofficially adopted daughter of Robert Wilson, one of the founders of the Keswick Meetings, a revival movement among Protestants in England.

She lived a full life of church work and one that was given fully to the Lord. For years she had been tortured over the fate of the heathen, though it did not occur to her that God might actually ask her to leave England and go to the missions. On January 13, 1892, God asked her to transform concern into action.

If she responded to the call, the human cost would be enormous. Her adopted father depended upon her companionship. Her mother relied on her as well. Amy's health would suffer in the tropics. Her leaving would be to them as if she had died, yet she knew she must go. Would those she loved be able to understand? On January 16, Mrs. Carmichael wrote back: "Yes, dearest Amy, He has lent you to me all these years. He only knows what a strength, comfort and joy you have been to me. . . . So, darling, when He asks you now to go away from within my reach, can I say nay? No, no, Amy, He is yours—you are His—to take you where He pleases and to use you as He pleases. I can trust you to Him and I do. . . . All day long He has helped me, and my heart unfailingly says, 'Go ye.' "[1]

Robert Wilson gave his blessing as well, but not without realizing the great loss and loneliness her departure would mean to him. A year later Amy sailed for Japan and became a member of a missionary group called the Japan Evangelistic Band. Always gifted with a flair for writing, she began to send home long monthly letters often illustrated with delicate drawings. This was a habit she kept up for the rest of her life. Despising the common approach of telling only upbeat news of missionary triumphs, Amy revealed the monotonous and discouraging side of it as well.

She lived and worked there for one year before succumbing to "Japanese Head," an illness that foreign missionaries were particularly prone to. She was forced to go to China for a long rest.

After a week in Singapore, Amy asked God what was next. "Go to Ceylon" was the answer. Amy sailed ten days later. So much for a long rest.

She quickly settled into a new routine and mission field. The work was promising but was interrupted ten months later when bad news came from England; her beloved "second father," Robert Wilson, had suffered a stroke. Amy sailed immediately for England, arriving in time for Christmas.

Mr. Wilson recovered. After ten months, on October 11, 1895, Amy departed again, this time to India. The climate, she assured her worried family and friends, would be much easier on her health. She never returned to England again.

India at that time had been under British rule for three hundred years. England had taken prodigious profits out of India but had given back some significant improvements in their place: the railway system, educational and governmental administration, and the judicial process. Still these benefits of Western civilization did not penetrate very deeply into the complex and multi-faceted culture of India. Administrators, soldiers, and missionaries often lived a totally British life in terms of comforts and society—largely separate from the native people.

This ease and insistence on living as English a life as possible appalled Amy: "If there were less of what seems like ease in our lives they would tell more for Christ and souls.... We profess to be strangers and pilgrims, seeking after a country of our own, yet we settle down in the most un-stranger-like fashion, exactly as if we were quite at home and meant to stay as long as we could. I don't wonder

Apostolic miracles have died. Apostolic living certainly has."[2]

Amy wanted to remove everything that separated her from the people. She found that her English clothes were unrealistic and distracting to the Indians. The logical solution to her was to wear a *sari*, but it just wasn't done. She rebelled against mandatory vacations for missionaries during the hottest time of the year. In time, she would refuse to take a furlough altogether, considering it a waste of God's time and discouraging others from taking one as well. She chose to travel from village to village and live in a tent, rather than a comfortable mission house. Whatever was radical and all-consuming naturally appealed to Amy.

On the other hand, older and wiser missionaries had difficulty persuading Amy to take sensible precautions and to be patient in her struggle to learn the Tamil language. But that was Amy.

With all her heart she desired to be Christ's radical disciple. The image of a soldier or warrior appears over and over in her writings and sayings. She saw every Christian, especially missionaries, as involved in a cosmic battle for the hearts and minds of men and women. She was there but for one purpose: to preach the gospel. She would allow nothing else to stand in the way and made every situation serve that goal.

She was zealous, impatient, and single-hearted, yet quick to make generalizations. Demanding on herself, she could expect more of others than was just. She had little tolerance for those less fervent in their faith. Brilliantly gifted and deeply committed, she needed the tempering of time in the mission field.

After fourteen months of studying Tamil, Amy was deemed competent enough to begin to evangelize. Mr. and Mrs. Thomas Walker were missionaries in the district of Tinnevelly affiliated with the Church Missionary Society. They invited Amy to join them in itinerant preaching from village to village. They traveled in springless, two-wheeled carts pulled by bullocks.

The small group was known as the "Starry Cluster." Several Indian women came to join Amy in the work: Ponnammal, or Gold; Blessing; Pearl; and Marial and her husband. They attempted to speak to the women, especially Brahman (the high caste) women.

The cost of becoming a Christian for men as well as women could easily mean death: an "accidental drowning," poison, or drugs administered that destroyed coherent thought. Baptism was never allowed. To choose Christ was to forsake one's home forever.

Two teenage girls, Ladychild and Jewel of Victory, decided for Christ and joined with the older women. For seven years Amy traveled from village to small town preaching the gospel. Her warrior's spirit was completely satisfied. She was doing the Lord's work.

A NEW UNDERSTANDING OF GOD'S WILL

At that point, Amy began to turn a corner that would revolutionize her understanding of God's plan for her life. On March 6, 1901, a seven-year-old girl, Preena, ran away from a temple where she was held against her will and straight into Amy's heart.

Hindu temples were served by *devadasis,* girls who were "married" to the god of the temple. They sang and danced before the god and prostituted themselves. Baby girls were bought and raised by temple women who trained them from their youth to be prostitutes. They were given a literary diet of erotic poetry to read—and Indian poetry is very explicit— until the scenes conveyed were natural and undisturbing. Example was part of their teaching as well.

Boys were also sold or given to the temple to become musicians and sacred dance instructors. Others were taught to act in obscene plays. Sexual exploitation came very early for many of these unfortunate children.

Ever since Amy had heard about this horrendous traffic in children, she had longed to do anything she could to stop it. Even so, she did not expect that "anything" meant her life would be consumed by mothering them herself!

Preena's mother had devoted her to the gods after her father's death. Preena ran away once and walked twenty miles home only to have her mother tear Preena's arms from around her neck and hand her back to the temple women. The women branded Preena's hands with hot irons as a punishment. They told her about the "child-stealing ammai," Amy, in order to frighten her. Preena, however, decided that this was just the one who could help her and ran away to find Amy.

It was exactly the right moment. Amy had just arrived in Pannaivali that evening. By the time an Indian woman found Preena it was too late in the day and too long a trip to bring her back to the temple. If Preena had run away any earlier, it would have been in vain. What was to become the major work of Amy's life began with God's perfect timing.

The next morning when Preena was brought to Amy the child ran right up to her and climbed into her lap. She had come to stay, she informed Amy, and Amy kissed her. In that moment Amy became *Amma*, mother. The temple women traced Preena and demanded that she be returned, but both Amy and the child refused.

The Starry Cluster became accustomed to having a small child around the house and began to delight in her. "I remember wakening up to the knowledge that there had been a very empty corner somewhere in me that the work had never been filled," Amy wrote. "And I remember, too, thanking God that it was not wrong to be comforted by the love of a child."[3]

Preena told Amy things about the life of temple children that horrified her. Victorian in upbringing, Amy could not even bring herself to say the word "leg." The outhouse was always referred to as "the place." The more she knew of the emotional and physical cruelty of the children, as well as the life of sexual slavery of temple women, the more she longed to save the children.

Three more children joined Preena, though they were not temple children. They were simply orphans who needed a mother and found one in Amy. The teenage girls—now numbering four—looked after the smaller children during the day when the older women were busy with their preaching and home visits. The same missionary band still traveled and camped outside the villages.

Eventually they began to call themselves a family and not a band. Family was not just a nice image for Amy but a reality. They were not running an orphanage; they were living together as a family.

It was harder to move from place to place with all the little ones in tow. Amy found it increasingly difficult to balance the tasks of evangelizing, caring for the women, girls, and children in the band, and continuing to hunt for more temple children. Even so, she could not accept giving up her ministry of preaching and evangelizing.

While in Japan, Amy had renounced all desire to be a wife and have a home of her own. She had chosen to be a missionary, so she struggled with trying to reconcile increasingly diverse demands on her time and energy. There was a Tamil proverb that said, "Children tie the mother's feet." Amy was beginning to see that she had to let her feet be tied for the sake of him whose feet were nailed for her.

Thomas Walker took over a class of divinity students at Dohnavur in 1905 for another missionary. The band went with him and settled in the vicinity, fully expecting to move on in a matter of months or even years. For three years, Amy and the Starry Cluster continued to travel, working out of a home base in Dohnavur. All the while they attempted to locate temple children.

One evening Amy had a vision of Christ praying in the garden of the bungalow for the children. It was his burden that he asked her to share with him, not her burden. At the same time, an Indian pastor in the northern part of the district was able to rescue a newborn from a temple woman. Within days, the tiny child was safe with the "Family" at Dohnavur. Preena was given the honor of naming her and chose Amethyst.

Another temple baby arrived in quick succession and was named Sapphire. Then an older child joined them in order to profess Christ. By June, 1905, the Family numbered seventeen children, of whom six were the fruit of years of prayer for temple children. By Christmas, they numbered thirty, including the adults.

As God added to their number, all aspects of the Family's life did not simply unfold neatly. They lived in buildings of sundried bricks with earthen floors and thatched roofs. The adults and older children had to take great effort and time to maintain them. There were constant termites. The floor had to be regularly treated with cow dung to harden the surface. The thatch posed the threat of fire as well. Washing machines, dryers, and electric stoves, of course, were non-existent. Food had to be cooked from scratch, flour ground, and rice husked. The amount of work was astronomical.

Indian life was ruled by caste. Caste determined who one would marry, how one would live, who one could talk to—including what work one would do. Even small tasks were divided by caste and rigidly adhered to. At first, recent converts would refuse to do work that was beneath their caste. This included much of the "motherwork" as Amy called it, of caring for babies. Amy would tolerate none of that. Washing feet was the task of the lowliest servant in the house at the time of Jesus, yet the Lord willingly did it for his disciples. With such an example, no task, however repulsive, was degrading for his followers, that even included changing diapers.

It was a lesson she herself had learned the hard way. Toward the end of her life, she mentioned to one of the workers that over the years she had cut thousands of little toenails. "I who said I would never do any work but 'preach the gospel.' It takes some of us years to learn what preaching the gospel means."[4]

MOTHERWORK AND LIFE IN THE FAMILY

It was difficult for her to give up her preconceived notions about missionary work and her role in God's plan. In fact, it took Amy several years to see that she must devote herself full-time to the Family. She learned that "motherwork" is no less in God's eyes than any other kind of work, no matter how spiritual in nature. If it is done in God's name, for his glory and toward his children, it is holy work. The goal, taken from the Keswick motto, was, *"Nothing less than to walk with God all day long."*

Amy wrote in *If*, one of her many books, "If by doing some work which the undiscerning consider 'not spiritual work' I can best help others, and I inwardly rebel, thinking it is the spiritual for which I crave, when in truth it is the interesting and exciting, then I know nothing of Calvary love."[5]

In a culture where social position was evident from what one could do or could not do based on race, this attitude was radical and challenging. By embracing this understanding, the women were able to break out of their caste mentality and truly be family with one another. Their focus was not on serving the children but on serving the Lord. They were family, first and last, and that meant that everyone had to take part in what was necessary to run a home.

Mrs. Carmichael, Amy's mother, came out to India in 1904 to help Amy. She immersed herself fully in the work of the compound. She was called *Atah*, grandmother, by the children, and they dearly loved her. She sewed and embroidered, taught English, and did what she could to help nurse and care for the babies.

A few weeks after her arrival, an epidemic struck, and all six babies died. Three months later Amy found out that Robert Wilson, her second father, had passed away on June 19. These losses wounded her loving heart deeply.

More babies came, and the work went on. Amy sent out monthly letters to an ever wider circle of friends.

Somehow in the midst of all her duties, she found time to write book after book, and sheaves of poems. It was a necessary outlet for her soul. Amy's writings reveal her spiritual growth and her valiant and faithful heart. They seem to be the arena where she wrestled with her worries, doubts, and desires until love became the victor. Her books are like a tapestry of what life in the Family meant. The obscure lives of ordinary people like Kohila, Ponnammal, Arulai are illuminated as infinitely precious in the eyes of God. A woman with a mother's heart wrote those books—a mother who loved her children and wanted others to love them as well.

Amy established a monthly day of prayer to intercede for all children in danger. During the month Family members would write out reasons for thanksgiving and put them in a Praise Box. On the Prayer Day, the box was opened and each reason read out loud so that all could give thanks together.

A branch nursery was established in Neyoor where there was a medical station run by the London Missionary Society. Fifteen of the most sickly babies lived there. Amy recognized the need for medical facilities and personnel. The Family began to pray for God to supply their wants in these areas.

Throughout her entire missionary career, Amy trusted God's providence to supply her needs directly. She did not believe in asking for donations or sending out appeal letters. If people asked how they could help, she was quick to tell them. But in all other cases she would ask God alone and wait on his answer. Many times the answer was miraculous.

She was convinced that prayer was essential for the work to continue. "... prayer is the core of our day. Take prayer out, and the day would collapse, would be pithless, a straw blown in the wind." It was evident from her monthly letters that God and our relationship with him alone was viewed as essential. Thus, for those who lived with her, prayer became like eating or breathing—a constant of life.

The other foundational principle of this most unusual family was the insistence that each person live in peace, without rancor and criticalness of each other. Loyal love was the root of the Family. Love was what families were all about. Love was what the Christian life was all about. When love did not triumph, Amy was deeply grieved. There were people who left Dohnavur in anger and dissension; not everyone agreed with her policies or decisions.

The Family grew and grew. Money, supplies, and personnel came as well. Dysentery swept through the nursery in 1907, and ten out of sixteen babies died. In 1913 seventy out of one hundred and forty members came down with malaria. Over the years, a hospital grew from an old hen house. Whimsically named Buckingham Palace, it grew into a real one that served the surrounding area. The staff to operate the hospital arrived as the medical facility expanded.

As her Family flourished, Amy's own character matured through the challenges she faced. She desired no earthly goods, but children need many things in order to be raised properly. Well, then, her own preferences must be laid aside.

August, 1912, brought the pain of four deaths in rapid succession: her spiritual mother in India, Mrs. Hopewood; a week later, one of Amy's favorite children, Lulla; exactly one week later, Thomas Walker; and then the following week, a girl of eight. A few months later, beloved Ponnammal, one of her tried and true companions since the first days of the "Starry Cluster," was diagnosed with cancer. The next July the redoubtable Mrs. Carmichael died as well.

Amy suffered terribly. She referred to these series of losses as the "lesson of the weaned child." Just as a child must learn to live without the milk which had fed him since birth, so Amy had to learn to do without the human support she had relied on. "There is only one way of victory over the bitterness and rage that come naturally to us—*To will what God wills brings peace.*"

LIFE IN THE COMPOUND

Life for Amy was a cosmic war in which each Christian was meant to be caught up in greater things of the Spirit. Radical living was the only way to respond. "Be the first wherever there is a sacrifice to be made, a self-denial to be practiced, or an impetus to be given," she told the children. It was the life she lived and the one she wanted for her children. To forget self and live for others was her goal for them.

She wrote to one worker's fiancée, "Dear, you are coming to a battlefield. You cannot spend too much time with Him alone. The keys of the powers of the world to come are not turned by careless fingers. So few are willing to pay the price of the knowledge of God. They play through life, even Christian life, even missionary life."[6]

One of the girls asked her what she should do when she grew up. "I pray that you will be a warrior and look after children," was Amy's reply. A great many of the girls did continue to work at Dohnavur and are still there to this day.

Motherhood and the call to be a warrior for Christ are not concepts that readily go together for most of us. But for Amy they were inseparable. All this military imagery can conjure up the picture of a stern, harsh, austere harridan, but that was not Amy at all.

As she grew older, she became plump. She loved to laugh

with the children and wrote scores of songs for them. In the early days, she would suddenly whisk them off to the seashore. The Family built homes in the mountains so they could take groups of children there in the hot season. Amy loved to ramble with the children through the jungle—a tea basket in tow—picnic beside waterfalls, and swim in deep, clear pools.

At first, before there were hundreds of children, Amy made every effort to kiss each child goodnight. Then she tried to see each child at least once each day. Since the children's birthdays were for the most part unknown, the day they came to Dohnavur was celebrated each year. Each child would be treated to breakfast with Amy and a chance to choose his or her own present from a large cupboard. Even toward the end, when there were almost nine hundred people in the Family and she was in great pain, Amy would write kind, little notes to keep in touch with as many of her little ones as possible.

Ponnammal, who had been Amy's choice as future leader of the Family, finally died from cancer in 1915. World War I affected their lives even though it was half a globe away, because it caused prices to skyrocket.

Amy and seven young Indian women from the Family "shaped themselves into a group" during these war years. They called themselves "Sisters of the Common Life." They learned English in order to read the spiritual masterpieces that gave strength to Amy's soul. Arulai even learned Greek in order to read the New Testament in its original language. Other women joined them. They were true daughters of Amy Carmichael.

Play and work were not separated, even the toddlers were put to work husking rice and cleaning their bungalows. As the children grew older, they learned to help with the younger ones. Faithfulness to duty was important. "A little thing is a little thing, but faithfulness in little things is a very great thing."

The children memorized Scripture and hymns. There was a schoolhouse on the compound. Sometimes the older ones taught the younger ones their basic drills in reading, writing, and arithmetic. They had their own fruit, flower, and vegetable gardens and sold the produce to the housekeeper. They were allowed to keep the money. Then once a year, as a group, they decided where to donate it.

Remembering the agony of long church services as a child, Amy kept Dohnavur's meetings to half an hour. She gave the youngest ones colored flags to wave during the singing, while the older ones played simple, rustic instruments.

As a mother, Amy did have drawbacks. Her Victorian upbringing gave her a narrow and unhealthy view of all sexual matters. Nothing was said about menstruation to the girls as they grew up. Brides were surprised on their wedding nights since no word was breathed beforehand. For the Family, though, there were remarkably few marriages. Finally, in the 1940s some of the younger missionaries insisted on teaching the children some form of sex education.

Amy did have favorites. According to some she preferred the light-skinned children to the darker ones. She doted in particular on several children over the years. Having favorites is something that most mothers will admit, but they usually insist that you never let the children know.

Education was rather old-fashioned. Later, when Dohnavur children attended higher schools, it was clear that their learning was deficient in some aspects. At first, Dohnavur children were even discouraged from going to college for fear they would abandon the call to serve others as they had been served. Only after India's independence and the passage of laws demanding certain degrees in higher education, did the policy change.

Of course, the inevitable happened. Some girls did rebel after tasting relative freedom outside the compound. Many of the present leaders at Dohnavur left for a time. Some even pursued careers away from home before returning.

Amy was willing to admit that she had made mistakes, and she desired to learn from them. Later in life, she studied some child psychology and decided to mix the age groups in the cottages for stability with their house mother or *accal.*

Amy's vision never stopped expanding. In 1931, the Family set about opening a dispensary to serve the people in a nearby town. On October 24, Amy went to Kalakadu, or as Amy renamed it, Joyous City, to inspect the house. It was almost dark before the key was found. Amy went to the newly-built outhouse. As she entered, she fell into the hole. It seems that the workers had dug it in the front of the shed, not out back as planned. As a result of the fall, her leg was broken, her ankle dislocated, and her spine twisted.

She never recovered from the injury. She was sixty-three years old and had neuralgia, heart trouble, hypertension, and was nearly blind in one eye. She found it difficult to sleep because of the pain. A bout with cystitis was overcome, but then neuritis set in. Her children insisted she sleep in a bed, instead of on the floor, and accept such luxuries as dusting powder for the heat. Like so many mothers who have served others all their lives, Amy now had to learn to let her children serve her. It was not easy.

Above the mirror in her bathroom were the words "Servant of All." She still sought ways to serve everyone she could. She wrote to other ill people. She wrote books with abandon, now that all possibility of manual work had been taken away.

Predictably, Amy tried the nerves of some of her nurses. But then again, she chose the girls who were most difficult to care for her. "Your last word will be one of pain," snapped one girl. Another threw a hot water bottle at Amy and ran away when Amy scolded her because she thought the girl had intentionally bumped the bed.

World War II troubled their lives, and donations dropped.

When it seemed as if Japan might invade, emergency evacuation plans were thought out and made ready, though they were never used. India won independence in 1947, but this event, which was so momentous for the country as a whole, did not have great impact on Dohnavur.

Amy could be demanding and inflexible if she thought it contradicted the "Pattern Shewn on the Mount," the plan she believed had been divinely revealed to her by God. No one else, it seemed, could hear God as well as she could.

Yet in her last years, she realized that Dohnavur was becoming rigid in the ways she had left it. No one, in fact, felt free to change a thing. She tried to retire, but they would not let her. Finally, leadership was formally passed on to her chosen successors.

After another fall, this one breaking her right arm and femur, her health began to deteriorate rapidly. In January, 1951, Amy fell into a coma. The whole Family—almost nine hundred of them—filed by her bed. On January 18, she slipped away, "carried by angels." Amy was buried on a pallet with a blanket of flowers under a tamarind tree. A bird bath with the one word *AMMAI*, mother, marks her grave.

Amy was a soldier, there's no doubt about that. But the war she waged was about being as loving and gentle and Christ-like as possible. She fought to win captives to Christ by love. Would that all parents fought such wars for their children's hearts and won.

✥ FOR YOUR LIFE ✥

- A Praise Box was instituted; family members were encouraged to write out reasons for thanking God on pieces of paper and drop the notes in the box. Once a month they were all read out loud.

- Amy taught the children that faithfulness in little things is very important.

- Motherwork was just as much preaching the gospel as evangelizing before an audience of hundreds.

- The children earned money and decided themselves what worthy cause to donate it to.

THIRTEEN

Challenged to Forgive
Assunta Goretti

Assunta Goretti is the only mother who has ever been present at her child's canonization. Her daughter died because she was faithful to her mother's teaching. Because of that teaching, she is, in a real sense, a saint as well.

TEENAGE ABDUCTIONS AND MURDERS are all too often the lead story on the evening news or in today's newspapers. Every locality, it seems, has its own lurid tale of a young girl or boy raped, missing, and then found dead. As parents, one of our greatest fears can be for our child's safety. Assunta Goretti experienced what so many of us fear: the violent murder of one of her children.

Her daughter Maria's heroic defense of her purity won her a martyr's death. Assunta was there as Maria died, and she lived to see her daughter canonized in 1950. Cardinal Salotti preached the sermon at Maria's beatification in 1947: "Without the teaching and example of her mother," he said, "Maria would never have been the heroic girl we know. After God and her own brave heart, all the merit goes to her mother." The crowds shouted, *"Vive le Mama! Vive le Mama!"* in response.

There is very little historical information about Assunta or her daughter, even though they lived during our century. Assunta Carlini was born in approximately 1866 but never knew her parents. She was raised by nuns in Senigallia, Italy, until she was five. After that she was shunted from one family to another, trading work for room and board. Unable to read or even sign her name, Assunta was among the poorest of the poor. She married Luigi Goretti in 1886 and had a son Tonino about a year later, but he died soon afterward. Another son, Angelo, was born two years later. Then in 1890 she had a daughter, Maria.

The Gorettis lived outside Corinaldo on a small plot of land that Luigi farmed. They had a home of their own but were very poor. Assunta had two more boys, Mariano and Alessandro, and a girl, Ersilia. As the family grew, Luigi could no longer support them, and they were forced to move to the Agro Romano where he became a tenant farmer. Here he became partners with Giovanni Serenelli and his sons Gaspar and Alessandro.

Life did not improve with the move. After a year, the Gorettis and the Serenellis moved to Ferriere de Conca to a larger farm. Their house was over the barn and stood stranded in the midst of the Pontine Marshes, a hotbed of malaria and typhoid fever. It was a deadly place to live and a horrible place to bring up a family. Both families had to share the same living quarters. Only absolute necessity could have made such a move possible. The children had no possibility of going to school, and Luigi had no time to teach them.

AN EDUCATION FOR ETERNAL LIFE

Assunta taught them the one necessary education for eternal life: to love God with all their hearts and to live for him each moment of the day. For her, the love of God was based on a profound reverence for his majesty. The children were taught to loathe sin because it would displease God. She told them Bible stories and the lives of the saints in the evening and sang to them as she worked. Assunta held up to them the ideal of becoming a saint. They prayed the rosary every night and went to Mass, even walking seven miles one way to the church at Nettuno.

Maria was about nine years old at the time of the move and was already a beautiful little girl, even though she was dressed in rags. Her beautiful hair, waist length and chestnut in color, particularly drew people's attention. Strangers as well as neighbors commented on her looks. This caused her mother a great deal of concern. Already it was very obvious that Maria was special: not only beautiful, kind, and loving but also intelligent and responsive to spiritual matters.

Because she realized that Maria's beauty would be the source of many temptations—both to Maria and to others—Assunta stressed purity of heart, mind, and action. Even in the hottest weather, Assunta would not dress in any way that could be construed as immodest, nor did her girls. Exactly what Maria knew about sex or how her mother told her is not known, but it is very clear that Assunta had taught her that it is a sacred gift and that her chastity pleased God and was worth protecting.

One day when she was eleven, Maria overheard a girlfriend of hers flirting with a boy near the well. She was horrified at the sexual innuendoes the two were trading back and forth. Maria filled the bucket and then hastened back home. She told her mother. "Why did you stay to listen?" Assunta demanded. "Let words like that go in one ear and out the other. You just make sure you never talk like that yourself."[1] Maria assured her that she would rather die first. Purity in speech, in dress, and action were an integral part of chastity for Assunta. To allow immodesty in one area would lead to impurity in all others.

On the other hand, Giovanni bought Alessandro, his eighteen-year-old son, pornographic magazines to read. The teenager cut out pictures and hung them on the wall of his bedroom.

Many intelligent men and women today deny that there is any link between pornography and the current rise in violent sex crimes. Like Ted Bundy of our half of the twentieth century, Alessandro would insist that they were wrong: the combination was deadly.

Two years after they moved to Ferriera de Conca, Luigi died of malaria. Assunta had to work in the fields in order to provide for the children. Maria took over her mother's duties as much as possible in the home, while Angelo helped as best he could around the farm. Maria watched the four younger ones including the baby, Teresa.

The elder Serenelli tyrannized the widow and her family. He locked the food cupboard and kept them half starved. Maria was expected to wash and mend both the Serenelli's clothes as well as her own family's and do the cooking for both families. Her mother, exhausted by the heavy farm labor, could not help her young daughter much. Maria had learned to do chores with her mother since she was a toddler. Assunta had kept her little ones at her side as she did her work, and now that training paid off. The ten-year-old was not perfect, especially in her cooking, but was able to do an adequate job. She especially excelled at caring for the children.

Assunta's chief desire at this time was that Maria prepare well for her First Holy Communion. It became a preoccupation for both of them during eleven months of lessons from a local catechist. Even after her teacher told her she was ready, Assunta was worried that Maria was not prepared enough. She asked the priest to test Maria's knowledge. Assunta believed that receiving Jesus in the Eucharist should make an observable difference in someone's life. Holiness of life and seriousness of intent were primary to her, and she passed those values on to her daughter. Even the smallest children made the long walk to Mass in order to teach them what it meant to be a good Christian.

As Maria prepared for this holy event, she entered into the unholy arena of temptation. Alessandro Serenelli began to try to seduce her whenever he found her alone. Finding that flattery got him nowhere, he tried to grab her and force her to kiss him on at least two different occasions. A mere kiss was not what he was after. She knew that well enough. Maria resisted and broke away from him. But he warned her, "If you tell your mother, I will kill you." Maria knew he meant it.

The two families were locked into the present arrangement and could not possibly split and go their separate ways until after the harvest. Maria truly believed that her mother would be utterly crushed by her death, so she kept silent out of love for her. She counted on the strength from Communion and the help of the Blessed Virgin to protect her. Only twelve years old, Maria remained watchful and stayed as close to her mother as she dared without making her suspicious.

On July 5, 1902, the Serenellis and Assunta and her boys were harvesting beans. They broke for lunch, and Alessandro told Maria to mend his shirt. She did not answer him and Assunta questioned her, "Don't you hear what he said?" Maria responded to her mother but ignored Alessandro. "Where is the shirt?"

Alessandro told her it was lying on his bed. As soon as she saw that he had walked back to the field, she dashed in, grabbed the shirt, and brought it out to the landing outside the door. She then settled baby Teresa down to nap on an old quilt and began her mending in full sight of her family working in the field.

Giovanni, exhausted and suffering from a fever, came to rest under the one tree in the area some distance from the door. He soon fell asleep. Shortly thereafter Alessandro

asked Assunta to drive his wagon because he had to go back
to the house to get something. Angelo drove the other cart,
and the younger children laughed happily and had a good
time.

When he entered the house, Alessandro took the stairs
two at a time and passed Maria without a word. He went
into his room, pulled out a dagger he had hidden, and went
into the kitchen. He pulled an old bench out, placed the
knife on top of it, went to the door, and then called Maria.
She suspected another trap and would not go in. "I will not
come in unless you tell me what you want," she insisted.

THE CALL TO MARTYRDOM

He stepped to the door. She stood up and gripped the
railing as hard as she could. Alessandro seized her arm and
wrenched her hands away, dragging her into the kitchen
before she could scream. He slammed the door shut and
locked it. Then Alessandro began pulling her dress off as she
struggled to get away from him. She shouted at him, "No,
no, no! What are you doing? You will go to hell! Do not touch
me. It is a sin." She fought him with a supernatural strength
for one so young.

Out on the landing, the baby woke up and finding herself
alone began to cry. But no one heard her over the threshing
and laughter out in the fields. Teresa cried louder.

Since she wouldn't relent, Alessandro stabbed Maria
again and again, and she screamed each time. Then Maria
fell to the floor. He thought she was dead and began to walk
away. "Oh my God! O God! I am dying," she sobbed.
"Mamma! Mamma!"

Alessandro's rage flared up again. He swung around and
grabbed her by the throat, stabbing her once more. This time
she was silent, and a small pool of blood began to form on the
floor. Satisfied, he went into his room, locked the door, and

threw himself face down on the bed.

Teresa was wailing now, and finally Assunta heard her. But where was Maria? She had been right there in plain sight but a moment ago. She yelled for her daughter, but there was no answer. Assunta told Mariano to go find Maria and find out why she had left the baby. Suddenly, she realized that Alessandro was gone as well and dread filled her mother's heart.

Meanwhile, Maria had dragged herself to the door and had tried to pull her clothes around her. Finally, she got the door unlocked and called out feebly, "Giovanni, come here! Your son has murdered me."

Giovanni rushed up the stairs and then shouted for Assunta and a neighbor, Mario Cimarelli, to come up as fast as they could. Other neighbors in the field saw the commotion and began to hurry to the house. Mario held Maria in his arms. The dress covered her wounds and at first Assunta did not realize what had happened; then she saw the blood on the floor and fainted. They laid Maria on the bed, and her godmother Teresa Cimarelli pulled back her torn dress, exposing her chest wounds. Maria came to and called for her mother. On the landing outside the house, Assunta—who had been taken outside—heard and broke away from those who tried to keep her back.

"Who did this to you, darling Maria?" she gasped.

"Alessandro. He wanted me to commit an ugly sin, but I would not, so he killed me." Then she passed out from the pain. The neighbors made Assunta go over to the Cimarelli's house until the ambulance came. Periodically, Maria would come to and whisper, "Poor Alessandro, you are going to hell!" Then she would shout, "Don't let him in here! Don't let Alessandro see me."

When the people realized Alessandro was still in the house, they rushed to the room and pounded on the door. But he did not answer. A hefty woman slammed into the door and knocked it open. Fortunately, the local police, the carabinieri, rescued Alessandro before he could be lynched by the mob. Once reinforcements arrived, they marched him to Nettuno to the jail.

Finally, the ambulance took Maria and her mother to the hospital. With every jolt over the rough roads, Maria's sufferings were intensified. Her mother could do nothing for her. On the way they passed the carabinieri and their prisoner. What were Assunta's thoughts as they passed her daughter's attacker, while the girl lay bleeding beside her? Nothing is recorded of any outbursts of hatred or promises of vengeance. Maria lay silently, stifling her moans, while her mother probably sat silently, choking back her anger and grief, concerned more about her daughter who needed her than the murderer who was left behind.

At the hospital the doctors took Maria immediately into surgery. They called for a priest also to come in and administer Last Rites. They knew it was hopeless, but they did their best to patch her up. Her lungs, heart, diaphragm, and abdomen had been pierced fourteen times. Because of the severity of her condition, she could not be sedated. Once out of the operating room and into a hospital room, Assunta was allowed to sit with her daughter.

Maria asked how her brothers and sisters were. She told her mother not to worry, that she was all right. They placed a picture of the Blessed Mother near her.

"I want to see my brothers and sisters once again," she asked her mother. But it was against hospital regulations, and Maria took the refusal peacefully.

The police interrogated her, and she had to tell the whole story over again. Meanwhile, Assunta sat beside her bed, knowing that her daughter was going to die. Maria drifted into silence. Then she cried out, "Alessandro, Alessandro, how unfortunate you are! You are going to hell!" She pleaded with her mother to keep him away from her.

As the hours passed, Maria became dehydrated and began begging for water. Her medical condition was so grave she could not have any. "I'm thirsty, I'm thirsty," she pleaded over and over. "Won't you give me even one drop of water?" Her daughter's pathetic cries for water haunted Assunta for years. The only comfort she had she offered to her daughter: Christ, too, was denied water on the cross and given vinegar instead.

The doctor ordered Assunta to leave at midnight. As she got up, Maria whispered in pain and anxiety, "Mamma, aren't you going to stay with me tonight?" Imagine the agony Assunta must have felt at that moment. Maria held on to her mother's hand, "But where will you sleep?"

Assunta found the ambulance was still there, so she slept in the back of it. In the morning Mario and Assunta waited outside the hospital for it to open. Some people passing by were talking in low voices, but Assunta heard the words, *"E morta!"* "The girl is dead." She fainted. When she came to, they pounded on the hospital door to find out for themselves. Assured that her daughter still lived, she hastened to Maria's bed.

The girl was very near death. Padre Girolamo asked her if she would like to be made a child of Mary, and he put the medal around her neck. He then asked her, "Remember, Maria, how Jesus forgave all those who condemned him to death and showed special mercy to the penitent thief? Do you remember that he said, 'Today you will be with me in Paradise?' Do you forgive your murderer with all your heart?"

Without hesitation she replied, "Yes, for the love of Jesus I forgive him. May he be with me in Paradise, and may God forgive him because I have already done so."

Assunta stayed by her side. She had taught her daughter to value purity and modesty above everything else. Little did she know it would exact such a cost from the two of them. Her daughter had been faithful to what she had been taught. Had she been wrong to set the standard so high? Would she have advised her daughter any differently if she had known the outcome? No. For the love of God, Maria clung to her purity. For the love of God, she now forgave her attacker. Martyrdom was the consequence of righteousness, and sainthood would be the affirmation of her mother's convictions.

As the afternoon wore on, Maria slipped in and out of consciousness. She called out for her father. Then she said to Assunta, "Forgive me, Mother," afraid she had caused her mother more sorrow by recalling her dead husband. She cried out for her mother, but Assunta directed her mind again to the Lord. "Pray for us, Maria, turn your heart to the Lord."

What did this cost the grieving mother? Wouldn't it have been so much more satisfying and consoling to let her daughter turn to her for comfort as she died? Wasn't it her right to hold her daughter's attention as she slipped into the next world? After all, God would have her all to himself forever, but they had only a few minutes left together. Assunta chose the harder path of self-denial. She denied her natural desires to be reassured of Maria's love, and focused instead on the condition of Maria's soul. Only a great-hearted woman would be capable of such a sacrifice.

As three o'clock approached, the time of her attack the day before, Maria grew frantic as she relived the horror again and prayed for her murderer. Then she died. "I was not worthy of such an angel," her mother groaned.

A MOTHER'S FORGIVENESS

The trial, in an ironic twist of fate, began on Maria's birthday, October 16. Alessandro showed no remorse and even flippantly said he killed her because he had a headache. He was sentenced to thirty years hard labor. Out of fear of retaliation by the infuriated townspeople, the authorities moved him by night to a prison in Sicily. For nearly eight years, he continued unrepentant and hard-hearted about the murder.

One night he dreamed of a garden where a beautiful girl with chestnut hair gathered lilies. She turned to look at him and he cried out. It was Maria. He shrank back, but her eyes were forgiving. She came to him and offered him her lilies. As he took them, they turned to flames in his arms, and she disappeared. When Alessandro awoke, he began to change. He eventually went to confession and repented for his sin.

Eighteen years later the Prison Board asked Assunta if she would give permission for Alessandro to be paroled four years early for good behavior. She assented.

On Christmas Eve in 1937, a gray haired man stood outside the rectory in Corinaldo. A seventy-three-year-old woman answered the door, and the man fell at her feet weeping. "Assunta, will you forgive me?" he begged.

Forgive him? The man whose father cheated the family of their living, starved them, forced her to do more than her share of work and who verbally insulted her daughter's cooking, washing, and mending time and time again? The man who tried to seduce her daughter while living in their home, who attempted to rape her, and then stabbed her fourteen times and left her for dead? Forgive him who had caused her beloved girl to suffer untold pain and thirst on her deathbed? Forgive him?

In tears, she answered him, "Maria forgave you, Alessandro; how could I not forgive you too?" She invited him inside, made him dinner, mended his clothes. Together they went to Midnight Mass, the murderer and the mother kneeling side by side.

There is a grace of martyrdom, they say, and it is a great one. By it Maria was able to transcend her fear of death and do what is right. She received the grace to forgive her attacker and by it soared to heaven. There must be a special grace for mothers who suffer the hidden martyrdom of loss and a most gracious gift of forgiveness for their children's oppressors. Assunta shared in both.

She taught her children to love God and to hate sin above all else. It was a path that led straight to martyrdom for her oldest daughter. We, too, need to teach our children to be honest, just, kind, chaste, and to love God above all else. If they are faithful to our teaching, they may one day lose their jobs, prestige, money, or even their lives. We may lose them to a far-off place as they live out their faith in service to the church. Or we may lose them to death. Virtue has a price for both child and mother.

It is a solemn responsibility we undertake to raise children for God, because they are called to live out what we teach them. We must pray all the more for the grace to mother our children and to suffer the consequences of their fidelity to the Lord.

We are in the serious business of raising a generation of possible saints. As mothers, we may have to drink the bitter cup of their sufferings with them, but we may also hope to share in their glory.

⚜ FOR YOUR LIFE ⚜

- Assunta saw purity as a whole way of life: speech, dress, thought, and actions must all be safeguarded for purity to be possible.

- She taught her children that sin displeases God.

- She impressed upon her children what a holy privilege it was to receive Jesus in the Eucharist.

- Assunta died to her own consolation and directed her daughter's thoughts away from her and toward God as her daughter lay dying.

- She accepted the grace to forgive her daughter's murderer.

Notes

ONE
"A Love Stronger than Death"
Maria Kolbe

1. All quotes are taken from Sr. Mary Felicita Zdrojewski's, C.S.S.F. excellent book *To Weave a Garment: The Story of Maria Dabrowska Kolbe, Mother of Saint Maximilian Maria Kolbe,* (Connecticut: Felician Sisters of the Order of Saint Francis of CT, Inc., 1989), 139.
2. Zdrojewski, 148.
3. Zdrojewski, 58.
4. Zdrojewski, 95.
5. Zdrojewski, 109.
6. Zdrojewski, 142-143.
7. Zdrojewski, 144-145.
8. Zdrojewski, 145.

TWO
"After God, It Was the Work of My Dear Mother"
Marie Vianney

1. All material in this chapter is common to any biography on St. John Vianney. Abbé Monnin's book, *Life of Saint John-Baptiste Vianney, the Curé d'Ars;* Abbé Francis Trochu's, *The Curé of Ars, St. Jean-Marie-Baptiste Vianney,* were the most relied upon. See the appendix entitled *Suggested Reading* for a listing of readily available books on St. John Vianney and his mother.

THREE
"I Was Born to Have Children"
Zélie Martin

1. All quotes are drawn from Zélie Martin's letters. As of yet, no collection in English exists. The source of longer quotes are given in the following pages.
2. Quoted in *The Story of a Family: The Home of The Little Flower*, by Stephane-Joseph Piat, O.F.M., (New York: P.J. Kennedy & Sons, 1948) 144.
3. Quoted in Dorothy Day's lively biography, *Thérèse* (Springfield, IL: Templegate Publishers, 1960, 1979), 25.
4. Piat, 35.
5. *The Autobiography of Saint Thérèse of Lisieux: The Story of a Soul*, trans. by John Beevers (New York: Image Books, 1957), 24.
6. I owe this insight to Hans Urs von Balthazar, *Thérèse of Lisieux: The Story of a Mission*, (New York: Sheed and Ward, 1954), 76.
7. Piat, 145.
8. St. Thérèse, *Autobiography*, 35.
9. Day, 54.
10. Piat, 198.
11. Day, 38-39.
12. Day, 39.
13. Piat, 238.
14. Piat, 279.
15. von Balthazar, 74, 75, 76.
16. St. Thérèse, *Autobiography*, 27.

FOUR
Birth in the Flesh and Spirit
St. Monica

1. All quotes are drawn from St. Augustine's *The Confessions*.

FIVE
The Mother of a Nation
St. Margaret of Scotland

1. E. Freeman, *History of the Norman Conquest* (Oxford: Clarendon Press, 1871), Vol. IV, 510.

2. A.M. Henderson-Howat, *The Life and Times of Saint Margaret of Scotland: Royal Pearl* (London: S.P.C.K., 1948), 75.
3. I owe this insight to Mrs. Henderson-Howat, op. cit. see 68-70.
4. Freeman, op. cit., 510.

SIX
She Brought Forth a Family of Saints
Alice of Montbar

1. The dream and advice Alice received are quoted in various forms in all the biographies of her son, Saint Bernard. This is a paraphrase of the version found in *Saint Bernard of Clairvaux*, translated by Geoffry Webb and Adrian Walker (Westminster, MD: The Newman Press, 1960).

SEVEN
Victor Over the Past
Barbe Acarie
(Beatified under Marie de l'Incarnation)

1. Lancelot C. Sheppard, *Barbe Acarie: Wife and Mystic*, (London: Burns & Oates, 1953), 146.
2. Henri Bremond, translated by K. L. Montgomery *A Literary History of Religious Thought in France*, Vol. II (New York: The MacMillan Co., 1930), 161-162.
3. Sheppard, op. cit., 136.
4. Ibid., p. 98.
5. Bremond, op. cit., 110-111.
6. Ibid., 107-108.
7. Sheppard, op. cit., 172.

EIGHT
Serenity in the Storm
Susanna Wesley

1. Luke Tymerman, *The Life and Times of the Rev. Samuel Wesley, M.A.* (London: Simpkin, Marshall and Co., 1866), 264.
2. Quoted in *Susanna Wesley*, Famous Women Series, by Eliza Clarke, (Boston: Robert Burns, 1886), 59.

222 / Mothers of the Saints

3. Adam Clarke, *Memoirs of the Wesley Family*, 2nd Edition (New York: Lane & Tippett, 1898), 328.
4. Adam Clarke, 326.
5. Adam Clarke, 111.
6. Adam Clarke, 328.

NINE

An Intensely Maternal Heart
St. Jeanne-Françoise de Chantal

1. Quoted in *Saint Chantal and the Foundation of the Visitation*, by Msgr. Bongaud (New York: Benzinger Bros., 1895) Vol. I, 240.
2. Bongaud, I, 238.
3. Bongaud, I, 242.
4. Bongaud, I, 242.
5. Bongaud, I, 197.
6. Bongaud, II, 43.
7. Bongaud, II, 290.
8. André Ravier, S.J., *Saint Jeanne de Chantal: Noble Lady, Holy Woman*, trans. Mary Emily Hamilton (San Francisco: Ignatius Press, 1989), 128.

A Mother for Life
Margarita Bosco

1. Many of the classic stories about Don Bosco's life are recounted in different versions in every biography. For the sake of simplicity all quotes or dreams are taken primarily from *Give Me Souls!: The Life of Don Bosco* by Pierre Lappin (New Rochelle: Don Bosco Publications, 1977/1988), 187-188.
2. Ibid., 27.
3. Ibid., 29.
4. Ibid., 31.
5. This dream is recounted somewhat differently in the preface to Lappin's book.
6. This is a paraphrase of several versions. One of them may be found in Lappin, 67.

7. Ibid., 66-67.
8. Ibid., 67.
9. Ibid., 76.
10. Ibid., 109.

ELEVEN
She Prepared Her Daughters to Die
St. Elizabeth Ann Seton

1. Quoted in *Elizabeth Bayley Seton 1774-1821* by Annabelle M. Melville (New York: Charles Scribner's Sons, 1951), 26.
2. Ibid., 44.
3. Quoted in Joseph I. Dirvin's *Mrs. Seton: Foundress of the American Sisters of Charity* (New York: Farrar, Straus and Giroux, 1962, 1972), 204.
4. Dirvin, 138.
5. Dirvin, 196.
6. Dirvin, 233.
7. Dirvin, 260.
8. Melville, 186.
9. Melville, 204.

TWELVE
"I Want You to Be a Warrior and Raise Children"
Amy Carmichael

1. Quoted in *A Chance to Die*, by Elisabeth Elliot (New Jersey: Fleming H. Revell Company, 1987), 55. This is by far the best and most comprehensive book on Amy Carmichael, and I strongly recommend it.
2. Elliot, 85.
3. Elliot, 165.
4. Elliot, 308.
5. Amy Carmichael, *If* (London: Society for the Promotion of Christian Knowledge), 43.
6. Elliot, 304.

THIRTEEN
Challenged to Forgive
Assunta Goretti

1. All quotes are based on two, often different, renditions of Assunta's, Maria's and Alessandro's words recorded in *Saint Maria Goretti* by Maria Cecilia Buehrle (Milwaukee: Bruce Pub. Co., 1950) and *Lily of the Marsh* by Alfred MacConastair, C.P. (New York: The MacMillan Co., 1951).

Suggested Reading

If you wish to read more about any of these mothers, you may find the following list helpful. Many books on these women are out of print or only available in a foreign-language edition. I have tried to include only books that can be found in most libraries or religious bookstores.

Madame Barbe Acarie

Lancelot C. Sheppard. *Barbe Acarie: Wife and Mystic.* London: Burns & Oates, 1953.

Alice of Montbar

Henri Daniel-Rops. *Bernard of Clairvaux.* trans. Elisabeth Abbott. N.Y.: Hawthorne Books, Inc., 1964.

M. Raymond, O.C.S.O. *The Family That Overtook Christ.* Boston, MA: St. Paul Editions, 1986.

Marie Bosco

Henri Ghéon. *The Secret of Saint John Bosco.* trans. F. J. Sheed. New York: Sheed & Ward Inc., 1936.

Peter Lappin. *Give Me Souls!: Life of Don Bosco.* New Rochelle: Don Bosco Multi-Media Publications, 1986.

Amy Carmichael

Frank Houghton. *Amy Carmichael of Dohnavur.* Fort Washington, PA: Christian Literature Crusade, 1979.

Elisabeth Elliot. *A Chance to Die: The Life & Legacy of Amy Carmichael.* New Jersey: Fleming H. Revell, 1987.

Elisabeth Elliot. "Amy Carmichael of India." *Heroes* Ann Arbor, MI: Servant Books, 1991.

St. Jeanne-Françoise de Chantal

André Ravier, S.J. *Saint Jeanne de Chantal: Noble Lady, Holy Woman.* trans. Mary Emily Hamilton. San Francisco: Ignatius Press, 1983.

Elisabeth Stopp. *Madame de Chantal: Portrait of a Saint.* Maryland: The Newman Press, 1963.

Assunta Goretti

Marie Cecilia Buehrle. *Saint Maria Goretti.* Milwaukee: Bruce Publishing, 1950.

Alfred MacConastair, C.P. *The Lily of the Marsh.* New York: The MacMillan Co., 1951.

Alicia von Stamitz. *Women of Valor.* Missouri: Liguori Publications, 1986.

Marie Kolbe

Mary Felicita Zdrojewski, C.S.S.F. *To Weave a Garment.* Connecticut: Felician Sisters of the Order of St. Francis of Connecticut, Inc., 1989.

Patricia Treece. *A Man for Others.* San Francisco: Harper and Row, 1982.

St. Margaret of Scotland

Henderson-Howat, A.M.D. *Royal Pearl: The Life and Times of Margaret Queen of Scotland.* London: S.P.C.K., 1948.

Zélie Martin

Beevers, John. *Saint Thérèse, The Little Flower: the Making of a Saint.* Rockford IL: Tan Books, 1976.

Beevers, John. *Storm of Glory: the Story of Saint Thérèse of Lisieux.* Garden City, NY: Image Books, 1955.

Day, Dorothy. *Thérèse.* Springfield, IL: Templegate, 1979.

Piat, Stéphane-Joseph. *Story of a Family.* New York: P.J. Kennedy, 1947.

Rohrbach, Peter-Thomas, O.C.D. *The Search for Saint Thérèse.* NY: Harmon House, 1961.

St. Monica

Augustine of Hippo, St. *The Confessions.* various translations.

Spark, Muriel. "St. Monica," *Saints and Ourselves.* ed. Philip Caraman, S.J. Ann Arbor, MI: Servant Books, 1983.

St. Elizabeth Ann Seton

Joseph Dirvin, C.M. *Mrs. Seton: Foundress of the American Sisters of Charity.* New York: Farrar, Straus and Giroux, 1962, 1975.

_____ *The Soul of Elizabeth Seton: A Spiritual Portrait.* San Francisco: Ignatius Press, 1990.

Annabelle M. Melville. *Elizabeth Bayley Seton 1774-1821.* New York: Charles Scribner's Sons, 1951.

Charles I. White, Rev. *Mother Seton: Mother of Many Daughters.* New York: Doubleday & Company, Inc., 1949.

Susanna Wesley

Rebecca Lamar Harmon. *Susanna, Mother of the Wesleys.* Nashville: Abingdon Press, 1968.

Marie Vianney

Monnin, Abbé Alfred. *Life of Saint John-Baptiste Vianney, Curé d'Ars*. London: Burns, Oates and Washbourne, LTD., 1926.

Sheppard, Lancelot C. *Portrait of a Parish Priest: St. John Vianney, the Curé d'Ars*. Maryland: The Newman Press, 1958.

Trochu, Abbé Francis Trochu. *The Curé of Ars, Saint Jean-Marie-Baptiste Vianney (1786-1859)*. trans. by Dom Ernest Graf, O.S.B. Maryland: The Newman Press, 1951.

Trouncer, Margaret. *Saint Jean-Marie Vianney: Curé d'Ars*. New York: Sheed & Ward, 1959.

Acknowledgments

The author and publisher wish to express their gratitude to the following for permission to reproduce material of which they are the authors, publishers, and/or copyright holders.

ONE Mary Felicita Zdrojewski, C.S.S.F., *To Weave a Garment*, (Enfield, CT: Felician Sisters of the Order of St. Francis of Connecticut, Inc.), © 1989 Felician Sisters of the Order of St. Francis of Connecticut, Inc.; select material reprinted with the publisher's permission.

THREE Dorothy Day, *Thérèse* (Springfield, IL: Templegate), © 1979 Dorothy Day; select material reprinted with publisher's permission.

TEN Peter Lappin, *Give Me Souls!: Life of Don Bosco* (New Rochelle, NY: Don Bosco Multi-Media Publications), revised edition © 1986 the Salesian Society; select material reprinted with publisher's permission.

ELEVEN Joseph Dirvin, C.M., *Mrs. Seton: Foundress of the American Sisters of Charity* (New York, NY: Farrar, Straus, and Giroux), © 1962 Farrar, Straus, and Giroux; select material reprinted with publisher's permission.

TWELVE Elisabeth Elliot, *A Chance to Die: The Life and Legacy of Amy Carmichael* (Old Tappan, NJ: Fleming H. Revell and Chosen Books), © 1987 Elisabeth Elliot; select material reprinted with publisher's permission.

While every effort has been made to trace copyright holders, several of the key source materials used are currently out of print and seem to be in the public domain. If there should be any error or omission, the publisher will be happy to rectify this at the first opportunity.

Also of Interest
from Servant Publications

St. Francis of Assisi
A Bibliography
By Omer Englebert

An acclaimed work of modern scholarship which is also
a timeless popular work of inspiring spiritual reading.
$5.95 (paperback)

The Little Flowers of St. Francis
*Incorporating the Acts of St. Francis
and His Companions.*
Translated by E.M. Blaiklock and A.C. Keys

A new translation of this popular, inspirational classic.
$4.95 (paperback)